PASTA
with a *Flair*

PASTA
with a *Flair*

By Katherine DeDomenico Reichert

Dillon Press, Inc. Minneapolis, Minnesota 55415

To my children
  Ralph, Janice, and Diane

Acknowledgments

Sincere thanks to the members of my family who contributed their recipes.

Special thanks to my daughter Janice for help with the recipes, typing, and computer work for the book.

Appreciation for all the assistance and advice from Home Economist, Catherine Dunlap.

Finally, to my husband, Ralph, thank you for the support, understanding, and love while writing my book. Your comments on the recipes were invaluable.

Food Stylist: Stevie Bass
Photographer: George Sellend

Library of Congress Cataloging in Publication Data

Reichert, Katherine DeDomenico.
  Pasta with a flair.

  1. Cookery (Macaroni) I. Title.
TX809.M17R44   1984   641.8′22   84-15635
ISBN 0-87518-283-6

Dillon Press, Inc., 242 Portland Avenue South
Minneapolis, Minnesota 55415
Printed in the United States of America

1 2 3 4 5 6 7 8 9 10 91 90 89 88 87 86 85 84

CONTENTS

CONTENTS

CONTENTS

MY BEGINNINGS

"I was born in San Francisco." To be able to make this statement has always made me feel proud. I love this city by the Golden Gate. One can see some of the most beautiful views in the world from the seven hills of San Francisco. From Chinatown to Fisherman's Wharf, from Ghirardelli Square to Golden Gate Park, San Francisco has many interesting places to see and visit.

I thank my father, Domenico DeDomenico, for having the foresight to live in such a fantastic city. This is his story as well as mine. My father immigrated from Messina, Italy, to the United States in 1888. He arrived in Boston, Massachusetts, and was greeted by an old friend from Messina. Together they went into business selling various products. Today they would probably be called brokers. After a few years in Boston, my father decided to go out West to San Francisco, where eventually he owned and operated three food markets.

Wanting a wife of Italian extraction who loved children as he did, my father asked his friends to help with the search. Maria Ferrigno was still living in Italy, but her uncle, who lived in San Francisco and knew my father, showed him Maria's photograph, and it was love at first sight. They corresponded, and he finally convinced her to come to this country in 1909. After eleven days of courtship they were married!

Mama had an unusual heritage. Her maternal grandparents had been in the pottery business in Vietri sul Mare, Italy, and had won 18 awards for designs in pottery. The Ferrigno side of the family had been in the macaroni business for generations; Mama's father had owned a macaroni factory. Early in their marriage, Mama convinced my father to go into the macaroni business. He sold his three markets and, in 1912, opened a small macaroni and spaghetti factory on Valencia Street in San Francisco. Using the Ferrigno family's formula for pasta, he named the company Gragnano Macaroni Factory. Gragnano was the name of a town in the mountains behind Sorrento where the finest macaroni products were made. My parents knew that their Italian-American customers would understand the meaning of that name. The company flourished and, in 1933, the name was changed to Golden Grain Macaroni Company. The factory grew through the years into one of America's major food industries. It is well known not only for pasta but for Rice-a-Roni and Noodle-Roni products.

My parents had six children, four boys and two girls, all of whom were born in San Francisco, California. I was the last one, the "baby" of the family. We lived in a modest Victorian house in the sunny Mission District. My fondest memories were our big, festive Sunday dinners with the dining room table fully extended and the family, relatives, and friends all eating Mama's very delicious cooking. Sometimes there were twenty or thirty people for dinner, but Mama never seemed to have had any trouble cooking for all of them. There would be an antipasto of olives, salami, and cheese, or oysters on the half shell. Then, there would always be a delicious pasta dish, chicken or leg of lamb, salad, and vegetables. Our favorite dessert was either cannoli (pastry shells stuffed with ricotta cheese, chocolate chips, and whipped cream) or Mama's cream pie made with vanilla custard and layered with wild cherries. Her crust tasted like a cookie.

When Mama made her own spaghetti sauce in the old days, my four brothers, sister, and I would ladle the sauce on french bread for our snack when we came home from school. It was so delicious. When my brothers decided to put Mama's sauce recipe in a can, the task became very frustrating. We all watched Mama cook, and just before she would add a "pinch" of this and a "fistful" of that into a pot, we'd ask her to relinquish the ingredient so we could measure the quantities. I had to do this with all the recipes that I received from her, as none of her recipes were written down. She relied on her memory for the right proportions and on her taste for the exact amount of herbs and spices. I learned to cook pasta dishes by watching Mama and imitating her. I was always in the kitchen, tasting her cooking before it was served. My biggest thrill was when my father complimented me the first time I made spaghetti and meatballs. He said, "Just like Mama's."

One day that will never be forgotten is December 7, 1941. On that particular day, Ralph Reichert had decided to ask my father for my hand in marriage. He was sitting at our dining table waiting to pop the question when over the radio came the news of the bombing of Pearl Harbor. Since Ralph was already in the military service, he knew he had to return to the base immediately, so he decided to ask the question. Naturally, my father was not in favor of a wedding with a war on, but we convinced him to reconsider, and we were married on January 25, 1942.

As the wife of a military man, I fully enjoyed my life traveling in the United States, Europe, and the Far East. My husband, Ralph, is a retired lieutenant colonel, USAF, and also retired military sales manager of Golden Grain Macaroni Company. We were blessed with three children — one son and two daughters.

My interest in good food and food preparation was enriched by traveling in Europe and the Far East. After my husband retired in 1961, we returned to California. At that time I began to share my interest and knowledge of culinary subjects with women's clubs and groups, giving them recipe ideas for the products manufactured by Golden Grain Macaroni Company. I was soon a welcome guest in high school home economics classes, where I demonstrated to future homemakers how to prepare the convenience foods.

One day my brother Vincent asked me to concentrate on pasta and do a pasta cooking demonstration. I gave my first cooking class, "Pasta — with a Flair," on March 1, 1978. My demonstrations are done in a specially designed stage kitchen that I helped create. The kitchen has special lighting and is attractively decorated with hanging plants, copper ware, cheese grater, and baskets. A large work center in the kitchen includes two electrical units, a portable sink, and two ovens. I travel with a complete portable kitchen, which provides me with all the pots and dishes I need for the demonstration. Incidentally, it takes a five-ton truck to haul my kitchen around! The pasta shows have been a very worthwhile and rewarding experience for me since they act as a service for the community. "Pasta — with a Flair" is offered to non-profit and charitable organizations for their fund-raising activities.

"Why don't you write a cookbook?" After hearing this question from cooking school audiences over the last six years, I have finally completed my collection — *Pasta with a Flair.* All the recipes have been tested and measured to give you the cup amounts so that you know exactly how many each recipe will serve.

In looking over the recipes you will notice that I use ingredients that are easy to find. Because everything is spelled out in clear detail, you should have great success with your pasta cooking. I feel that this is why my demonstrations have been so well received. I assure you that you will be proud to serve any recipe in this book for I have not omitted any secret ingredients.

PASTA — PAST AND PRESENT

Pasta is one of the oldest foods in the world. In Italy, it dates back to 5000 B.C. Although pasta was not actually discovered by Marco Polo, most historians agree that this food's popularity dates from the time of the Venetian traveler's return from China, which coincides with the beginning of the Italian Renaissance. The cooking of the Italian peninsula was the first fully developed cuisine in Europe, and pasta was its principal staple. Italians loved pasta so much that they actually wrote poems in its praise. One seventeenth-century Neapolitan poet, Scruttendio, wrote a sweet poem to his beloved:

"My dear little Cecca, she gave me a plate
Of macaroni delicious with a taste that was great.
All sprinkled with sugar and cinnamon round about,
So good when I ate it I almost passed out."

Italy has always been and still is the largest consumer of pasta products in the world. Two towns near Naples, Gragnano and Torre Annunziata, were famous for the best pasta made in Italy. Outside a pasta factory, the street would be lined with endless racks strung with spaghetti drying in the sun. Drying pasta in the sun wasn't that easy. Luckily, these towns had the best climatic conditions for drying pasta. Here the hot winds blew off the volcano Vesuvius, alternating with the fresh breezes from the Mediterranean Sea. There couldn't have been more perfect conditions.

In America, pasta is as old as the Republic. Thomas Jefferson introduced pasta in 1786 after his return from a long stay abroad, as ambassador to France. He brought back a spaghetti-making machine and a die to make pasta for his family and friends. Pasta products first appeared commercially in 1848 in Brooklyn, New York.

Pasta means *dough* in Italian. An amazing variety of pasta has come down through the years. The best pasta is made from the same basic ingredient — hard durum wheat. Although there are hundreds of varieties of wheat, the one of outstanding significance is Triticum durum, or durum wheat, sometimes known as macaroni wheat. This unique variety has a high yield per acre and is resistant to drought and rust, a disease caused by parasitic fungi. Durum (meaning hard) wheat is high in protein (gluten), and has an intense yellow amber color. This wheat is much harder than the red Spring and hard red Winter wheats, and is planted in the spring and harvested at the end of August.

In the United States, about 85 percent of durum wheat is grown in North Dakota. Smaller amounts are grown in Minnesota, Montana, South Dakota, and California. Through government, universities, and private industry, research is going on all the time to improve the strains of durum wheat. Researchers are looking for higher yields, better rust resistance, greater disease and insect resistance, and necessary gluten quality.

A complicated process of milling converts the durum wheat kernel into semolina and durum flour by removing all unnecessary particles and grains. From a simple mixture of semolina and water, pasta is made. Egg noodle products have frozen or dry eggs added. Before shipping to the manufacturer, the semolina is enriched with the essential B vitamins — thiamine, riboflavin, niacin — and the mineral, iron.

The great increase in production of macaroni products has been made possible by the inventions of automatic presses and driers. The manufacturers of macaroni and noodle machinery are continually improving and modifying production equipment.

There are two methods of manufacturing macaroni products. One is the batch process, and the other is the continuous press. The continuous process, which is widely used throughout the world today, is completely automatic and saves labor costs. Various devices are used for measuring semolina, water, dough consistency, kneading, and drying. The dough accumulates in a small chamber, and when the space is filled, the dough is extruded through a bronze metal plate with holes, called a die. The amount of pressure through the different dies creates the various pasta curves and shapes. A pin or a steel rod in the center of the die forms the hold in a macaroni that is tube shaped. The automatic spreader places strands of extruded spaghetti on drying sticks, which are automatically conveyed into the dryer. Short pasta and noodle products are spread onto belts and then into the dryer. Drying is done in several stages. The objective is to alternately dry the surface, then let the product rest. In this way the moisture inside the pasta can come to the surface. If pasta is dried improperly or very quickly, it will crack. If it dries too slowly, pasta will become moldy. After drying pasta is automatically weighed, packaged, and delivered to your store. Macaroni products must be stored in a cool, dry place.

Today over two-hundred different pasta shapes are available to the consumer. Fettuccine, linguine, mostaccioli, rigatoni, and zitoni are just a few. Golden Grain makes about fifty of the more practical and popular shapes. Each shape tastes best when used with special sauces or recipes as you will notice when you try the recipes in this book.

PASTA IS GOOD FOOD

Pasta is one of the simplest foods, and yet it can assume a hundred different tastes. Such a versatile food, pasta can be an appetizer, a main dish, a side dish, or even a dessert. Besides tasting so good, pasta is also economical.

There are five healthy reasons to add pasta to your diet: no salt, no sugar, no fat added, no artificial preservatives, and no artificial coloring or flavoring. Pasta is a good food because it is easily digested, assimilated, and absorbed. Complex carbohydrates such as bread, rice, and pasta are recommended today to maintain a healthy and energetic body.

Pasta is a kind of "time release" food. The carbohydrates, vitamins, and minerals of pasta metabolize slowly, serving as fuels for the body over an extended period. With foods like pasta, a chemical reaction takes place in the body. First the long starch molecules are broken down into smaller starch molecules and finally into simple sugars, specifically glucose, for energy. Glucose, composed of a six-carbon chain, is the ultimate food for the brain as well as for muscle activity. Glucose is stored in muscle tissue and liver as glycogen. When you need added energy, another chemical reaction occurs, which converts the glycogen to glucose.

Many people think that pasta is fattening. A look at the caloric content will clear up this misconception. One gram of carbohydrate yields four calories, while one gram of fat provides more than twice that amount — nine calories. We need to give up the idea of pasta being fattening and enjoy this very healthy and nutritious food.

SO EASY TO COOK

Pasta products are really quite simple to prepare, but a lot of people have trouble cooking this food. The difficulty usually results from trying to cook pasta in a pot that is too small or not using enough water. To cook from 12 to 16 ounces of pasta requires at least 5 quarts of water. The smallest pot you should use is a 6-quart saucepot. The pasta must float freely in the water in order to cook properly.

Once the water is brought to a rolling boil, salt is added. Since many people today are on salt-free diets, salt is an optional ingredient. If you do use salt, add 1 tablespoon to 5 quarts of water or according to taste. Slowly add your pasta to the boiling water and stir gently until the water returns to a boil. Sometimes I cover the saucepot temporarily with a lid to let it return to a boil more quickly. I do not start timing until the water starts boiling again. Add one tablespoon of vegetable oil, if desired. Adding the oil will prevent the water from boiling over, which is a problem most pasta cooks must contend with.

Pasta products should be cooked to the firm but tender stage, which is called *al dente* or "firm to the tooth." If you happen to like your pasta a little softer, you can add 1 to 3 minutes to the cooking time but usually not any longer. When the pasta is done to taste, connoisseurs, who like their pasta cooked "just so," can pour a cup of cold water or some ice cubes into the boiling water to halt the cooking process.

Make sure the colander you use to drain the pasta has lots of holes on the sides and bottom. Water trapped in the colander will dilute the sauce.

Premium quality pasta, like Golden Grain, should only be rinsed if you are going to cool it for a macaroni salad. If you are using the pasta for a salad, rinse the pasta in cold water and drain it well to prevent the pasta from sticking together. Add salad ingredients and refrigerate. When you want to cook pasta ahead of time, rinse it in cold water and drain it well. When the pasta is cool, add one tablespoon vegetable oil and work the oil through the pasta. Cover with plastic wrap and refrigerate until you need it. To reheat cooked pasta, add the pasta to 5 quarts of boiling water, stir, and heat for 2 minutes. The water does not need to boil again as the pasta is already cooked. Drain and serve. If you are filling cooked pasta or deep frying it, be sure to pat the pasta dry with paper towels before filling or frying. Except for salads when the macaroni is rinsed in cold water, pasta should just be drained well and served with your favorite sauce.

When reheating a pasta casserole or leftovers, I find it helpful to sprinkle a little water, or milk if it is a milk based dish, over the pasta. The liquid makes the leftovers taste even better.

Pasta cooked, drained, and tossed with butter and Parmesan cheese is one of our family favorites. My grandchildren just love this dish. You can add as much butter and Parmesan cheese as you like, so I'll not give you a recipe for this dish.

Godere! Enjoy!

FRITTATA DI PASTA

Delicious as a leftover pasta dish and ideal for a Sunday brunch, this egg dish can be frozen and reheated.

1 cup cooked spaghetti or leftover pasta
3 eggs
1/4 cup grated Parmesan cheese
1/4 pound Italian sausage, cooked and sliced
4 ounces Monterey Jack cheese, shredded
1 tablespoon sausage drippings
Orange slices and parsley for garnish

Cut cold, cooked spaghetti into small pieces. Beat eggs; stir in spaghetti, Parmesan cheese, sausage, and Monterey Jack cheese. Heat sausage drippings in an 8-inch, nonstick skillet; pour in spaghetti mixture. Fry 5 minutes or until brown and crisp. Slide out of pan onto flat plate; invert the skillet over plate and reverse. Fry the other side for 5 minutes. Garnish with orange slices, cut in half, and parsley. Cool 5 minutes. Makes 4 servings.

THE ELEGANT EGG

SPAGHETTI ALLA CARBONARA

Here is a traditional recipe for carbonara.

> **1/2 pound sliced bacon, cut in 1/4 inch pieces**
> **4 eggs**
> **1/4 teaspoon pepper**
> **3 tablespoons bacon fat**
> **1 package (16 ounces) spaghetti**
> **Grated Parmesan cheese**

Fry bacon until crisp, reserving 3 tablespoons bacon fat. Beat eggs until foamy. Add pepper and bacon fat. Cook spaghetti according to package directions; drain. Pour egg mixture onto platter. Toss with hot spaghetti and bacon pieces. Serve with Parmesan cheese. Makes 6 (1 cup) servings.

CREAMY CARBONARA

I once tasted a dish like this in Rome, where they used pancetta (Italian bacon). Outstanding!

1/2 pound sliced bacon
4 eggs
1 cup whipping cream
3 tablespoons bacon drippings
1/4 teaspoon salt
1/4 teaspoon pepper
1 package (16 ounces) vermicelli
1/2 cup grated Parmesan cheese

Fry bacon until crisp, reserving 3 tablespoons bacon drippings. When cool, break the bacon into pieces. Beat eggs in serving bowl until foamy. Add cream, bacon drippings, salt, and pepper; stir together. Cook vermicelli according to package directions; drain. Warm egg mixture in a 250°F oven while vermicelli is cooking. Toss vermicelli with egg mixture, Parmesan cheese, and bacon pieces. Makes 6 (1-1/4 cup) servings.

CARBONARA PARMIGIANO

Additional Parmesan accents the cheese flavor in the carbonara.

1/2 pound sliced bacon, cut into 1/4 inch pieces
1 package (12 ounces) egg tagliarini
3 eggs
Salt and pepper
1/4 cup minced parsley
3/4 cup grated Parmesan cheese

Fry bacon until crisp; reserve drippings. Cook egg tagliarini according to package directions; drain. Beat eggs with salt and pepper until fluffy; stir in parsley and cheese. On a platter, toss egg tagliarini with bacon and drippings. Fold in egg mixture. Makes 6 (1-1/4 cup) servings.

FRITTATA DI VERDURA

Here is a frittata for vegetarians.

1/2 pound (2 cups) zucchini, sliced
1/2 cup chopped onions
2 tablespoons olive oil
3 eggs
1 cup cooked vermicelli, cut into small pieces
1/4 teaspoon salt
1/8 teaspoon pepper
1/4 cup grated Parmesan cheese
1 teaspoon olive oil

Sauté zucchini and onions in 2 tablespoons olive oil for 10 to 15 minutes until crisp-tender. Beat eggs; stir in vermicelli, zucchini mixture, salt, pepper, and Parmesan cheese. Heat 1 teaspoon olive oil in an 8-inch, nonstick skillet on medium heat. Pour in zucchini mixture and fry for 3 to 4 minutes or until brown and crisp. Slide out of pan onto flat plate; invert the skillet over plate and reverse. Fry the other side for 3 to 4 minutes. Cool 5 minutes. Makes 4 servings.

SOUP POT SUPPERS

MAMA'S MEATBALL MACARONI SOUP

I love this soup. My husband could eat the whole potful. If you use canned chicken stock, use either 4 (14-1/2 ounces) cans or 1 large can (49-1/2 ounces) and dilute with 2 cups cold water. Don't add more salt. Add pepper to taste.

Meatballs
1 (2 inch) piece stale sourdough French bread
1/2 pound ground beef
1 egg
1/4 cup finely chopped parsley
1/2 teaspoon salt
1/4 teaspoon pepper
1/4 cup grated dry Monterey Jack or Parmesan cheese

Soak French bread in cold water until soft. Remove crust and squeeze out water; tear into pieces, about 1/2 cup. Combine all ingredients and roll into small meatballs. Makes approximately 20-30 meatballs, depending on size.

Soup
1/2 cup chopped onion
2 tablespoons butter
8 cups chicken stock
1/4 cup finely chopped parsley
Salt and pepper
1 cup sea shells
Grated, dry Monterey Jack or Parmesan cheese
Parsley

Sauté onion in butter. Stir in chicken stock, parsley, and salt and pepper to taste. Bring to boil; add meatballs to soup. Return to boil, add sea shells, and boil 15 minutes. Top with dry Monterey Jack cheese and parsley. Makes 8 (1 cup) servings.

MEATBALL LENTIL SOUP

My brother Tom's wife, Lois, is a great cook and entertains often. Her culinary talent blends well with her involvement in community service activities, where she gives a lot of time and effort to fund-raising events. This recipe is one of her favorites.

1 pound lentils
2-1/2 quarts cold water
2 teaspoons salt
1 teaspoon pepper
1/2 cup butter
1 can (28 ounces) tomatoes
1 large onion, minced
1 teaspoon dry dill weed
1/2 teaspoon marjoram
4 cloves garlic, minced
2 bay leaves
1 pound ground lamb
1 teaspoon salt
1/4 teaspoon pepper
1 egg, beaten
1 tablespoon flour
1 tablespoon oil
1 cup elbow macaroni

Early in the day, wash lentils and place in saucepot with next ten ingredients. Cook, covered, over low heat for 1 hour. Combine lamb with salt, pepper, and egg. Form into 24 balls; roll in flour and brown in hot oil. Add meatballs and elbow macaroni to soup; bring to boil and cook 30 minutes. Makes 8 (2 cup) servings.

PASTA PISELLI SOUP

My niece Joan loves to cook and entertain. She reminded me of this old family favorite. Pasta piselli is an inexpensive and tasty soup.

> 1 large onion, minced
> 4 tablespoons oil
> 4 cups chicken broth
> 1 package (10 ounces) frozen petite peas
> 1/2 teaspoon salt
> 1/2 teaspoon pepper
> 1/2 package (8 ounces) salad macaroni
> Grated Parmesan cheese

Sauté onion in oil. Using a 2-quart saucepan, add chicken broth, peas, salt, and pepper; cook for 15 minutes. Cook salad macaroni in 2 quarts boiling water with 2 teaspoons salt for 10 minutes; drain. Add to soup mixture. Serve in soup bowls, topped with Parmesan cheese. Makes 4 (2 cup) servings.

ITALIAN MINESTRONE SOUP

I have always enjoyed this make-ahead soup my daughter Diane serves on busy days.

2 stalks celery, chopped
1 large onion, chopped
1 leek, chopped
1 clove garlic, crushed
1/2 cup minced parsley
1-1/2 teaspoons dried sweet basil leaves
3 tablespoons olive oil
2 carrots, sliced
2 potatoes, cubed
1 medium turnip, cubed
3 medium zucchini, cubed
1/4 small head cabbage, shredded
1 cup fresh shelled peas or
    1 package (10 ounces) frozen peas
1 can (16 ounces) stewed tomatoes
4 cans (14-1/2 ounces each) beef broth
1 can (14-1/2 ounces) kidney beans
1 cup sea shells
Salt and pepper
Grated Parmesan cheese

In a 6-quart saucepot, saute celery, onion, leek, garlic, parsley, and basil in olive oil about 5 minutes. Add carrots, potatoes, turnip, zucchini, cabbage, and peas. Sauté 10 minutes, stirring occasionally. Stir in stewed tomatoes and beef broth; bring to boil. Reduce heat, cover, and simmer 45 minutes, stirring occasionally. Stir in kidney beans and sea shells; cover and cook approximately 20 minutes until sea shells are tender. Salt and pepper to taste. Top with Parmesan cheese. Makes 8 (2 cup) servings.

RED SEA CLAM CHOWDER

Made with macaroni shells, this chowder is rich, red, and delicious.

6 slices bacon, diced
1/2 cup chopped onion
1 cup chopped celery
1 clove garlic, minced
1 can (28 ounces) tomatoes
1 cup water
1 can (12 ounces) tomato vegetable juice
1 bottle (8 ounces) clam juice
1 teaspoon salt
1/8 teaspoon pepper
2 cups large shell macaroni
2 cans (6-1/2 ounces each) chopped clams
1/4 cup minced parsley

Sauté bacon 5 minutes; add onion, celery, and garlic. Cook until bacon is brown. Add tomatoes, water, vegetable juice, clam juice, salt, and pepper. Bring to a boil. Stir in shell macaroni and cook, covered, for 20 minutes. Stir occasionally until shell macaroni is tender. Add clams and parsley; simmer 5 minutes. Makes 6 (1-1/2 cup) servings.

SOUP POT SUPPERS

QUICK EGG DROP SOUP ITALIAN

My sister, Jean, reminded me of this very delicious soup Mama used to make. We all loved it. Jean believes it is so satisfying and nourishing, all you need to add is a green salad for a nice lunch or dinner.

2 quarts water
2 teaspoons salt
1 large onion, thinly sliced
1 large tomato, cut into small pieces
1/2 cup chopped parsley
3 tablespoons oil
1/2 package (8 ounces) salad macaroni
4 eggs
3 tablespoons grated Parmesan cheese
Salt and pepper

In 2 quarts of boiling, salted water, cook onion, tomato, and parsley for 10 minutes. Add oil and salad macaroni into rapidly boiling water, stirring slowly. Cook for 10 minutes. Do not remove any water from pot. Scramble 4 eggs with Parmesan cheese; salt and pepper to taste. Add scrambled eggs slowly into salad macaroni, continually stirring until cooked.

This is a thick soup. If soup seems too thick, add more hot water and salt to taste. Makes 5 (2 cup) servings.

SEA SHELL CLAM CHOWDER

I have included this recipe for lovers of white clam chowder!

4 slices bacon, diced
1/2 cup chopped onion
1 cup chopped celery
2 cups water
3/4 teaspoon salt
1/8 teaspoon pepper
1 cup sea shell macaroni
1 can (8 ounces) minced clams
2 cups milk
1 tablespoon minced parsley

Sauté bacon for 5 minutes. Stir in the onion and celery and cook 5 minutes longer. Add water, salt, and pepper and bring to a boil; stir in sea shell macaroni. Cover and boil for 12 minutes, stirring once during cooking time. Add the clams, milk, and parsley. Simmer for 5 minutes. Makes 4 (1 cup) servings.

CAPELLINI VEGETABLE SOUP

My niece Debbie loves to cook and really enjoys making soup. A busy person, she still takes time to do pasta dishes.

1-1/2 cups coarsely chopped onions
3/4 cup leeks (white part only)
6 cloves garlic, minced
1 medium turnip, cubed
1 medium rutabaga, cubed
2 medium white potatoes, cubed
8 ounces medium mushrooms, cut in thick slices
4 carrots, cut into 1/4-inch slices
3 tablespoons butter
1 can (28 ounces) peeled tomatoes, drained and cut up
9 cups chicken broth or stock
8 ounces fresh spinach (tear into 2-inch pieces)
2 cups coil capellini, broken up
1 teaspoon salt
Pepper
1 tablespoon olive oil (optional)
1 pound Kielbasa, cut in 1/2-inch slices (optional)

Wash and prepare vegetables. Melt butter in large, heavy saucepot over medium heat. Add onions, leeks, and garlic; sauté 2 to 3 minutes. Add turnip, rutabaga, potatoes, mushrooms, and carrots; cook about 3 minutes, stirring frequently. Increase heat to high, add tomatoes and chicken broth and bring to boil. Reduce heat and simmer, covered, about 8 to 10 minutes until vegetables are crisp-tender. Increase heat; add spinach, coil capellini, salt, and pepper to taste. Cook for 5 minutes, or until pasta is tender. Heat olive oil in frying pan and sauté Kielbasa, stirring frequently until browned, 3 to 5 minutes. Remove with slotted spoon and drain on paper towels. Add Kielbasa to soup; adjust seasoning if necessary. Makes 8 (2 cup) servings.

BEEF VEGETABLE SOUP

My husband, Ralph, is retired and enjoys making soups, using some of his homegrown vegetables. This one he especially likes.

2 pounds beef shanks (center cut)
4 quarts cold water
2 beef bouillon cubes
1 cup cubed green pepper
1 cup cubed celery
1-1/2 cups cubed carrots
2-1/2 cups cubed zucchini
1 cup cubed white onion
1 cup shredded cabbage
2 cups sliced mushrooms
1 can (8 ounces) tomato sauce
Salt and pepper
1-1/2 cups salad macaroni or sea shells
Grated Parmesan cheese

Put beef shanks in 4 quarts of cold water and bring to a boil. Add bouillon cubes and simmer, covered, for 1 hour. Add vegetables, tomato sauce, salt and pepper to taste. Cook until all vegetables are tender, about 1/2 hour. In separate pot, cook salad macaroni according to package directions; drain. Add macaroni to soup. Top with Parmesan cheese. Makes 10 (2 cup) servings.

MAMA'S MINESTRONE SOUP

Mama's recipe for minestrone is thick with vegetables, and, truly, a meal in itself.

1/2 pound ground beef
2 tablespoons olive oil
1/2 cup chopped onions
1 cup diced celery
1 clove garlic, minced
1 can (29 ounces) tomatoes, cut up
6 cups water
2 beef bouillon cubes
1 teaspoon salt
1/4 teaspoon black pepper
2 teaspoons oregano leaves
1 can (15-1/4 ounces) kidney beans, drained
2 cups diced zucchini
2 tablespoons chopped fresh parsley
2 cups rigatoni
Grated Parmesan cheese

Brown ground beef in olive oil. Add onions, celery, and garlic and sauté until soft. Add tomatoes and water and bring to boil. Add remaining ingredients, except rigatoni and cheese. Bring back to boil; add rigatoni. Cook 15 to 17 minutes, or until rigatoni is tender, stirring occasionally. Top soup generously with Parmesan cheese. Makes 11 (1 cup) servings.

LENTIL SOUP

My daughter Janice's husband, Ed, loves to eat this soup with French bread.

1-1/2 pounds ham hocks
2-1/2 quarts cold water
1 package (12 ounces) lentils, rinsed
1/2 cup chopped carrots
3/4 cup diced celery
3/4 cup chopped onions
1 teaspoon salt
1/4 teaspoon pepper
1/2 cup minced parsley
1 cup salad macaroni

In a 6-quart saucepot, bring ham hocks, water, and lentils to a boil. Add carrots, celery, onions, salt, pepper, and parsley. Simmer for 2 hours, stirring occasionally. After soup has cooked for 1-1/2 hours, cook salad macaroni according to package directions; drain. Add macaroni to lentil soup and stir. Remove ham hocks; cut ham in small pieces; discard the rind and return ham to soup. Makes 8 (2 cup) servings.

SUMMER SALADS

MACARONI FRUIT SALAD

Fruit with pasta makes a very delicious and refreshing salad. What a perfect meal for hot summer evenings!

8 ounces elbow macaroni
2 teaspoons salt
1 tablespoon instant minced onions
1/2 cup sour cream
1/2 cup salad dressing
1 teaspoon salt
1/4 teaspoon cinnamon
1 tablespoon lemon juice
1 can (8 ounces) crushed pineapple
1 can (11 ounces) Mandarin oranges, drained
1 red apple, cut into chunks
1/2 cup sliced celery
1/2 cup flaked coconut
1/2 cup chopped nuts

Add elbow macaroni, 2 teaspoons salt, and 1 tablespoon instant minced onions to 3 quarts rapidly boiling water. Cook macaroni according to package directions. Drain and rinse with cold water. Blend together sour cream, salad dressing, 1 teaspoon salt, cinnamon, and lemon juice. Combine macaroni with dressing; add remaining ingredients and mix together. Chill. Makes 12 (3/4 cup) servings.

PESTO SALAD

This recipe is the same as Vermicelli al Pesto (page 124) but served cold as a salad with the twistee egg noodles. Hot or cold, both pesto dishes are great!

1 package (12 ounces) twistee egg nooldes
1 cup packed, fresh spinach leaves
1/2 cup packed parsley leaves
2 tablespoons dried sweet basil leaves
1 cup Bertolli olive oil
2 cloves garlic
1/2 cup pine nuts or walnuts
1 teaspoon salt
1/2 teaspoon pepper
3/4 cup grated Parmesan cheese

Cook twistee noodles according to package directions. Rinse in cold water until cold; drain. Combine remaining ingredients in food processor or blender. Blend until smooth. Toss pasta with pesto. Makes 9 (1 cup) servings.

MACARONI SALAD DIJON

This macaroni salad is very pretty and easy to make. The touch of mustard and capers makes it exotic.

1/2 package (8 ounces) elbow macaroni
1 cup red pepper strips
2-1/4 ounces sliced ripe olives, drained
1 package (4 ounces) boiled ham, cut into strips,
    2 inches long
2 tablespoons capers, drained
2 tablespoons chopped parsley

Dressing
6 tablespoons olive oil
2 tablespoons lemon juice
1 tablespoon grated Parmesan cheese
1-1/2 teaspoon Dijon mustard
1/4 teaspoon salt
1/8 teaspoon pepper

Cook elbow macaroni according to package directions. Rinse in cold water until cold; drain. Add red pepper, ripe olives, ham, capers, and parsley. Combine dressing ingredients; beat well with wire whisk and add to salad. Toss and chill. Makes 9 (1 cup) servings.

BARBECUE MACARONI SALAD

This salad is so delicious. When my children were growing up, they loved it so much they used to eat the salad as a snack. It keeps a week in the refrigerator and tastes better day by day.

1 package (16 ounces) salad macaroni
1 can (7-3/4 ounces) marinara sauce
1-1/2 cups chopped celery
1 cup sweet pickle relish
1 can (4 ounces) chopped ripe olives
1/2 teaspoon chili powder
1-1/2 cups mayonnaise
1/2 cup minced onions
Salt and pepper

Cook macaroni according to package directions; drain. Rinse with cold water. Combine macaroni, marinara sauce, celery, relish, olives, and chili powder. Chill overnight. Just before serving, stir in mayonnaise and onions. Salt and pepper to taste. Makes 9 (1 cup) servings.

SPRING GARDEN PASTA SALAD

This spring salad is absolutely beautiful and delightful. When asparagus is not in season, substitute 1 package (8 ounces) frozen, cut up asparagus.

Olive oil and wine vinegar dressing
        6 tablespoons olive oil
        4 tablespoons white wine vinegar
        1-1/2 teaspoons Dijon mustard
        1/2 teaspoon salt
        1/4 teaspoon pepper
        1 clove garlic, minced
        1 teaspoon dried sweet basil leaves

Salad Ingredients
        6 ounces asparagus, cut in 1-inch pieces
        1/2 cup cubed red pepper
        1/2 cup cubed green pepper
        2 tablespoons chopped parsley
        1 cup shredded provolone cheese
        1/2 package (6 ounces) medium egg noodles
        1/2 package (5 ounces) frozen peas

Combine dressing ingredients. Cut up asparagus, red and green pepper, parsley, and cheese. Cook noodles according to package directions. During the last 6 minutes of cooking, add asparagus. Last 2 minutes add frozen peas; drain. Rinse pasta and vegetables until cool. Combine remaining vegetables, cheese, and parsley. Toss with dressing. Chill. Makes 6 (1 cup) servings.

TUNA AND BROCCOLI ROTELLE SALAD

The family nutritionist is my niece Vicki. She gave me this recipe for a delectable, colorful salad using tuna. It should be made just before you are ready to eat.

3/4 cup olive oil
2 tablespoons dried sweet basil leaves
1 tablespoon lemon juice
1/4 teaspoon grated lemon peel
2 cloves garlic, minced
3 tablespoons chopped parsley
1 package (12 ounces) rotelle
2 cups broccoli flowerettes
3 cups fresh tomatoes, peeled and cut in thin wedges
1/2 cup sliced green onions
1 can (6-3/4 ounces) water packed, solid white tuna
    (albacore), well drained
1/2 cup grated Parmesan cheese
Salt and pepper

Whisk olive oil, basil, lemon juice, lemon peel, garlic, and parsley together. Set aside so that spices become soft and flavorful. Cook rotelle according to package directions, adding broccoli during the last 5 minutes of cooking; drain. Rinse in cold water to stop the cooking process. Toss rotelle/broccoli with olive oil dressing until pasta is well coated. Add tomatoes, green onions, tuna, and Parmesan cheese and toss again. Salt and pepper to taste. Makes 11 (1 cup) servings.

PASTA BUFFET SALAD

Neapolitans love mostaccioli. This pasta is an unusual shape for a party salad.

Salad Dressing
      2/3 cup walnut oil
      1/2 cup white wine vinegar
      3 teaspoons Dijon mustard
      1 teaspoon salt
      1/2 teaspoon pepper
      2 cloves garlic, minced
      2 teaspoons dried sweet basil leaves

Salad Ingredients
      1 package (10 ounces) frozen petite peas, cooked
      1 package (12 ounces) mostaccioli
      1/2 large red onion, sliced
      1 can (2-1/4 ounces) sliced ripe olives
      1 jar (4 ounces) sliced pimientos
      4 ounces sliced ham or mortadella, cut in strips

Prepare salad dressing. Cook mostaccioli according to package directions; drain. Rinse with cold water. Combine pasta with salad dressing, cooked peas, onion, olives, pimientos, and ham. Chill. Makes 10 (1 cup) servings.

PICNIC MACARONI SALAD

This salad tastes best when chilled overnight and is an easy macaroni salad to prepare.

1 package (12 ounces) sea shells
1/4 cup instant chopped onions
1/4 cup salad oil
1/4 cup wine vinegar
1 teaspoon salt
1/4 teaspoon black pepper
1/2 teaspoon dill weed
1/2 cup Miracle Whip salad dressing
1/2 cup mayonnaise
1 tablespoon prepared mustard
1-1/2 cups chopped celery
3 hard-cooked eggs, chopped
1/4 cup chopped parsley
1/2 cup minced onions

Cook sea shells with instant onions according to package directions; drain. Rinse with cold water. Whisk together salad oil, wine vinegar, salt, pepper, and dill weed. Toss with cooked pasta and chill for at least 30 minutes. Blend salad dressing, mayonnaise, and mustard. Combine dressing and remaining ingredients with sea shells. Chill. Makes 9 (1 cup) servings.

JUST A LITTLE MEAT

MAMA'S SWISS STEAK, ITALIAN STYLE

Easy to make, Mama's swiss steak is a satisfying meal. Add a salad and your meal is complete.

1 pound round steak, cut into pieces
3 tablespoons flour
1 teaspoon salt
1/4 teaspoon pepper
3 tablespoons oil
3/4 cup chopped onion
2 cans (15 ounces each) marinara sauce
1/2 cup red wine or water
2 cups sliced celery
1 cup green pepper strips
1 package (12 ounces) medium egg noodles

Dredge steak with mixture of flour, salt, and pepper. Brown in hot oil. Stir in onions and sauté. Add marinara sauce and wine; bring to boil. Add celery and green pepper. Simmer, covered, 45 minutes or until meat is tender. Cook noodles according to package directions; drain. Serve sauce over noodles. Makes 6 (1-3/4 cup) servings.

MAMA'S SPAGHETTI AND MEATBALLS

When Mama made meatballs, she always poured a little red wine in a small bowl. She would then dip her fingers in the bowl and wet the palm of one hand with the wine and roll the meat into balls so each meatball received a caress of wine. Delicious! I handle meatballs the same way, but, of course, this touch is optional.

1 piece (4 inches) stale sourdough bread
1 pound lean ground beef
1/2 cup grated Parmesan cheese
1/2 cup finely chopped parsley
2 eggs
1 teaspoon salt
1/2 teaspoon pepper
2 tablespoons olive oil
1 jar (32 ounces) marinara sauce
1/2 cup dry vermouth
2 dashes cinnamon (optional)
1 package (16 ounces) spaghetti
Grated Parmesan cheese

Soak bread in cold water. Remove crust, squeeze water from bread, and tear into small pieces (approximately 3/4 cup). Combine bread, beef, Parmesan cheese, parsley, eggs, salt, and pepper. Shape into 1-1/2-inch meatballs. Brown in oil; drain. Add marinara sauce, dry vermouth, and cinnamon to meatballs and simmer 30 minutes.

Cook spaghetti according to package directions; drain. Serve meatballs with sauce over spaghetti. Sprinkle with Parmesan cheese. Makes 6 (1-2/3 cup) servings.

ITALIAN POT ROAST

Mama liked to cook a roast in her own sauce. Probably the Arab influence in Italy made Mama always add cinnamon to her pasta sauce. I love the taste of cinnamon, which makes the sauce sweet.

1 tablespoon butter
2 tablespoons olive oil
3-1/2 to 4 pounds boneless, cross rib roast
1 cup chopped onion
1 can (14-1/2 ounces) whole peeled tomatoes, cut up
1 can (8 ounces) tomato sauce
1 can (6 ounces) tomato paste
1-1/2 cups water (or 1/2 cup red wine and 1 cup water)
2 cloves garlic, minced
1 teaspoon salt
1/2 teaspoon black pepper
1/4 teaspoon cinnamon
1/4 teaspoon allspice
1/2 teaspoon sugar
1 package (16 ounces) cut macaroni
Grated Parmesan cheese

Heat butter and olive oil in Dutch oven or large saucepot. Brown roast on all sides over medium heat. Remove roast, add onions, and sauté until soft. Add tomatoes, tomato sauce, tomato paste, and water; bring to boil. Add garlic, salt, pepper, cinnamon, allspice, and sugar. Stir and return roast to pot. Cover and simmer 3 hours, turning roast occasionally.

Cook cut macaroni according to package directions; drain. Top with sauce and Parmesan cheese. Slice roast and serve with pasta. Makes 8 servings.

PASTA WITH STUFFED STEAK

Braciola Ripieno is the Italian name for this dish, but I thought stuffed steak tells exactly what it is. My sister-in-law Lois gave me this delicious recipe, which is perfect for company.

>1/2 cup minced parsley
>4 cloves garlic, finely chopped
>1 cup grated Parmesan cheese
>1 pinch salt
>1/2 teaspoon pepper
>2 pounds boneless sirloin, sliced into 4 very thin steaks
>Lightweight cotton string
>1/4 cup olive oil
>1/2 cup Florio Dry Marsala wine
>2 cans (15 ounces each) marinara sauce
>1 package (16 ounces) cut macaroni

Mix parsley, garlic, cheese, salt, and pepper. Spread evenly over 4 steaks. Roll each steak and tie with string so that filling doesn't come out. Heat olive oil in a 4-quart saucepot. Brown steaks over medium-high heat. Add wine and marinara sauce. Simmer 45 minutes or until tender.

Cook cut macaroni according to package directions; drain. Remove steaks from sauce and remove string; slice into 1/2-inch slices. Pour sauce over macaroni and top with sliced steak. Makes 5 servings.

VERMICELLI PEASANT STYLE

Don't let the name fool you. Vermicelli Peasant Style is a quick dish to make, but so delectable.

>1/4 pound mushrooms, sliced
>1 clove garlic
>6 tablespoons butter
>1 package (12 ounces) vermicelli
>1/4 pound sliced prosciutto or ham, cut in pieces
>1/2 package (5 ounces) frozen petite peas, thawed
>1 cup whipping cream
>Salt and pepper
>Grated Parmesan cheese

Sauté mushrooms and garlic in 4 tablespoons of butter for about 5 minutes. Cook vermicelli according to package directions; drain. Add prosciutto and peas to mushrooms and cook another 5 minutes, stirring constantly. Remove garlic clove; add cream and heat. Salt and pepper to taste. Toss vermicelli with remaining butter, then sauce. Sprinkle with Parmesan cheese. Makes 5 (1-1/3 cup) servings.

SICILIAN SAUSAGE ZITONI

My father was Sicilian and loved the spicy taste of sausage in his pasta dishes.

1/2 pound mild Italian sausage, cased
1 tablespoon olive oil
3/4 cup green pepper strips
3/4 cup sliced mushrooms
1/2 cup onion strips
1 jar (32 ounces) marinara sauce
1 package (12 ounces) zitoni
Grated Parmesan cheese (optional)

Brown sausage in oil. Remove from skillet and slice. Sauté green pepper, mushrooms, and onions. Add marinara sauce and sausage; simmer 15 minutes. Cook zitoni according to package directions; drain. Serve sauce over zitoni and top with Parmesan cheese, if desired. Makes 4 (2 cup) servings.

STRAW AND HAY

The combination of spinach and egg fettuccine gave this popular name to this recipe.

1/2 cup chopped onion
1 clove garlic, minced
4 tablespoons butter
6 ounces pancetta (Italian bacon), sliced thin and diced
1/2 pound mushrooms, sliced
1-1/2 cups half and half
1 teaspoon dried sweet basil leaves
Dash of nutmeg
Pepper
1/2 package (5 ounces) fettuccine
1/2 package (5 ounces) spinach fettuccine
1/2 cup grated Parmesan cheese

In skillet sauté onion and garlic in butter until soft but not browned. Stir in pancetta and mushrooms and sauté 5 minutes. Add half and half, basil, and nutmeg and cook for 5 minutes. Add pepper to taste. Set aside. Cook fettuccine and spinach fettuccine according to package directions; drain. Toss fettuccine in skillet with pancetta and mushroom sauce; add Parmesan cheese. Makes 6 (1 cup) servings.

JUST A LITTLE MEAT

NORTH BEACH RIGATONI

Vegetables, sausage, and pasta are three foods Italians love. This dish is a complete meal in itself and very simple, as you can be simmering the vegetables while your pasta is cooking.

> 1 pound Italian sweet sausage links
> 1 large onion, cut in wedges and separated
> 1 medium green pepper, cut in strips and halved
> 1 pound zucchini, cut in 1/2 inch slices
> 1/2 pound mushrooms, cut in half
> 1/4 cup Florio Dry Marsala wine
> 1/2 teaspoon salt
> 1/4 teaspoon pepper
> 1 can (15 ounces) marinara sauce
> 1 package (12 ounces) rigatoni
> 1/2 pound Bel Paese, sliced thin, or Monterey Jack
>   cheese, grated

Brown whole sausages in a 4-quart saucepot until thoroughly cooked. Remove sausages, cool, and slice in 1/4-inch slices. In sausage drippings, sauté onion and green pepper until crisp-tender. Add zucchini, mushrooms, wine, salt, pepper, marinara sauce, and sausages. Simmer 14 minutes. Cook rigatoni according to package directions; drain. Turn into large bowl. Top rigatoni with cheese, then hot sauce. Makes 6 (2 cup) servings.

ITALIAN STYLE RIGATONI

Here is another version of the Italian favorite.

> **1 pound Italian sausage**
> **1 cup chopped onion**
> **2 cloves garlic, minced**
> **1 can (28 ounces) tomatoes, chopped**
> **1 can (8 ounces) tomato sauce**
> **1/2 teaspoon salt**
> **1 tablespoon olive oil**
> **2 tablespoons chopped parsley**
> **1 package (12 ounces) rigatoni**
> **Grated Parmesan cheese**

Remove sausage from casing; brown with onion and garlic. Add tomatoes, tomato sauce, salt, oil, and parsley. Bring to boil; simmer, uncovered, 15 minutes. Cook rigatoni according to package directions; drain. Serve with sauce. Top with Parmesan cheese. Makes 6 (1-1/3 cup) servings.

ZUCCHINI MESCOLANZA

Zucchini is a versatile vegetable, which is perfect with pasta and ground beef.

1/2 pound ground beef
1 cup chopped onion
1 clove garlic, minced
3 cups sliced zucchini
2 cans (15 ounces each) marinara sauce
1 can (2-1/4 ounces) sliced ripe olives, drained
1 teaspoon salt
1/4 teaspoon pepper
1 package (12 ounces) mostaccioli
Grated Parmesan cheese (optional)

Cook ground beef, onion, and garlic until light brown. Add zucchini, marinara sauce, olives, salt, and pepper; simmer for 10 minutes or until zucchini is tender. Cook mostaccioli according to package directions; drain. Serve mostaccioli with zucchini sauce. Garnish with Parmesan cheese, if desired. Makes 6 (2 cup) servings.

VEAL SCALOPPINI WITH MOSTACCIOLI

My daughter Janice is my chief assistant and understudy for my cooking school. Veal Scaloppini is her family's favorite, which always gets an enthusiastic response.

1-1/2 to 2 pounds veal cutlet, thinly sliced
1/2 cup flour
1/2 teaspoon salt
1/4 teaspoon pepper
4 tablespoons butter
1/2 cup chopped green onions
1 cup sliced, fresh mushrooms
1 clove garlic, cut in half
Pinch sweet basil leaves
1 can (14-1/2 ounces) stewed tomatoes
1 can (15 ounces) marinara sauce
1 cup Florio Dry Marsala wine
1 package (12 ounces) mostaccioli
Grated Parmesan cheese (optional)

Cut veal into 3-inch squares; pound. Dredge with seasoned flour. Brown in 2 tablespoons butter; set aside. Add remaining 2 tablespoons butter to skillet; add green onions and mushrooms and sauté about 3 minutes. Add garlic, basil, stewed tomatoes, marinara sauce, and wine and mix well. Add browned veal to skillet and simmer, covered, for 25 minutes. Cook mostaccioli according to package directions; drain. Remove garlic. Serve sauce and veal over mostaccioli. Sprinkle with Parmesan cheese, if desired. Makes 6 servings.

CALIFORNIA TAMALE PIE

This Mexican dish includes a pasta and is a favorite of people in the San Francisco Bay Area.

2 cups (8 ounces) elbow macaroni
1 pound ground beef
1 cup chopped onion
1 clove garlic, minced
1 can (28 ounces) tomatoes
1 can (8 ounces) tomato sauce
2 tablespoons chili powder
1-1/2 teaspoons salt
1/4 teaspoon pepper
12 ounces grated Cheddar cheese
1 cup green pepper strips
1 can (8-3/4 ounces) corn, drained
1 can (8-3/4 ounces) kidney beans, drained
3/4 cup pitted ripe olives, halved
1 package (6 ounces) corn chips (long, curly)

Cook elbow macaroni according to package directions; drain. Brown ground beef, onions, and garlic. Add tomatoes, tomato sauce, chili powder, salt, and pepper. Simmer 10 minutes. Stir in cooked elbow macaroni, half the cheese, green pepper, corn, beans, and olives. Layer 4 ounces of corn chips and meat mixture in a 3-quart, oblong baking dish. Top with remaining cheese and chips. Bake at 400°F for 15 minutes. Serves 8.

RIGATONI SUPREMA

This rigatoni dish is an exotic recipe created by my sister-in-law Mildred. You'll love it.

1/2 pound veal stew meat, cut in small cubes
1/2 cup chopped parsley
1 carrot, cut in 4 pieces
1 bay leaf
2 ounces salt pork
2 tablespoons olive oil
4 to 6 green onions, sliced
1/4 pound prosciutto, chopped
1 package (9 ounces) frozen artichoke hearts, cooked
4 tablespoons tomato paste
1/4 cup dry sherry
1/2 cup veal stock or chicken broth
1-1/4 pounds rigatoni
1/4 pound mushrooms, sliced
1 cup frozen peas, cooked
1-1/2 cups whipping cream
Salt and pepper
Grated Parmesan cheese

Cook veal with parsley, carrot, and bay leaf for approximately 1 hour in enough water to cover veal. Add more water if needed. Drain and reserve stock. Put salt pork in cold water and heat to boil without lid. Boil 2 minutes to get rid of excess salt. Cut in small pieces and sauté in olive oil. Add green onion, prosciutto, artichoke hearts, and cooked veal and sauté until green onions are limp and cooked, about 3 minutes. Add tomato paste, sherry, and veal stock and mix well. Simmer 7 minutes.

Cook rigatoni according to package directions; drain. Add mushroom and peas to veal mixture and simmer 5 more minutes. Add cream; stir and heat but do not boil. Salt and pepper to taste. Toss rigatoni with sauce. Serve on platter and sprinkle with Parmesan cheese. Makes 6 (2 cup) servings.

THE CHICKEN TRADITION

CHICKEN CACCIATORE

An elegant recipe, chicken cacciatore will receive raves from family and friends.

Salt and pepper
3 pounds chicken pieces
1/4 cup olive oil
2 cups (1/2 pound) thickly sliced mushrooms
1 green pepper, diced
1 jar (32 ounces) marinara sauce
1/2 cup Florio Dry Marsala wine
1 package (12 ounces) twistee egg noodles

Salt and pepper chicken; brown in oil and remove from pan. Add mushrooms and green pepper; sauté 3 minutes. Add marinara sauce, wine, and chicken. Simmer, covered, for 45 minutes. Cook twistee noodles according to package directions; drain. Serve sauce and chicken over twistees. Makes 6 servings.

CACCIATORE MOSTACCIOLI

I've always enjoyed this recipe. The chicken makes the sauce so light and gives it an outstanding flavor.

1/2 cup flour
2 teaspoons salt
3 pound frying chicken, cut up
1/2 cup oil
1/4 cup chopped onion
1 clove garlic, chopped
1/4 cup chopped carrot (optional)
Few sprigs parsley
1 bay leaf (optional)
1 can (28 ounces) whole tomatoes
Salt and pepper
1/4 cup sherry or white wine
1 package (12 ounces) mostaccioli

Sift flour and one teaspoon salt together. Dredge chicken parts with flour. Sauté in oil until brown. Place in covered dish and keep hot. Using same oil, sauté onion, garlic, carrot, parsley, and bay leaf in a large saucepot. Add cut up tomatoes and juice, pepper, and one teaspoon salt to sautéed vegetables. Bring to a boil. Add chicken and wine. Simmer about 30 minutes.

Cook mostaccioli according to package directions; drain. Place in serving dish. Pour sauce over mostaccioli and arrange chicken on top. Makes 6 servings.

TURKEY SCALOPPINI

You will find this turkey dish a nice change from veal, and more economical.

1/2 cup flour
1 teaspoon garlic powder
1/2 teaspoon salt
1/2 teaspoon pepper
1 pound turkey breast, cut in thin slices
6 tablespoons butter
1 medium onion, chopped
1 can (14-1/2 ounces) chicken broth
1 cup dry vermouth or white wine
1 can (8 ounces) mushrooms, pieces and stems, drained
1/2 teaspoon garlic powder
1 tablespoon lemon juice
1/2 teaspoon thyme, crushed
1/2 teaspoon salt
1/4 teaspoon pepper
1 cup sour cream
1 package (12 ounces) medium egg noodles
Parsley, chopped for garnish

Combine flour, garlic powder, salt, and pepper. Reserve 2 tablespoons flour mixture for sauce. Coat turkey slices well with flour mixture and sauté in butter until brown. Remove from pan and keep warm. For sauce, add onion to pan and sauté for 2 minutes. Stir in 2 tablespoons reserved flour mixture, mixing well. Add broth, wine, mushrooms, garlic powder, lemon juice, thyme, salt, and pepper and simmer until sauce thickens slightly. Remove from heat and whisk in sour cream.

Cook noodles according to package directions; drain. In a 3-quart casserole, layer 1/2 of sauce mixture, noodles, and remaining sauce. Top with cooked turkey and garnish with chopped parsley. Makes 6 servings.

SLOW COOKER CHICKEN

This outstanding chicken dish was given to me by my niece Joyce. The additions of pancetta and Marsala wine give the chicken that exotic flavor.

3-1/2 pounds chicken, cut up
1/2 cup flour
1/2 teaspoon salt
1/4 teaspoon pepper
1/2 teaspoon garlic powder
2 tablespoons olive oil
4 tablespoons butter
1/4 pound pancetta (Italian bacon), 1/4-inch slices, cubed
1 medium onion, thinly sliced
1/2 pound mushrooms, sliced
1 can (28 ounces) tomatoes with juice, cut up
1/2 teaspoon oregano
1/2 cup freshly chopped parsley
3/4 cup Florio Dry Marsala wine
1 can (15 ounces) marinara sauce
1 package (12 ounces) egg spaghettini
Grated Parmesan cheese (optional)

Set 5-quart slow cooker on high and turn on. Coat chicken with combined flour, salt, pepper, and garlic powder. Heat olive oil and 2 tablespoons of butter in large frying pan and brown chicken on both sides. Place chicken in slow cooker. Sauté pancetta 3 minutes in frying pan; add onions and mushrooms and cook until soft. Put pancetta, onions, mushrooms, tomatoes, oregano, parsley, and wine in 5-quart slow cooker. Stir and mix thoroughly. Cover and cook on high, approximately 4 hours. Stir occasionally. Last half hour of cooking chicken, add 1 can of marinara sauce.

Cook egg spaghettini according to package directions; drain. Toss pasta with remaining 2 tablespoons melted butter. Individually spoon spaghettini, sauce, and chicken on dish. Sprinkle with Parmesan cheese, if desired. Makes 6 servings.

EGG TAGLIARINI WITH CHICKEN LIVERS SAUTÉ

This tasty recipe is simply thin strands of egg noodles with a flavorful sauce.

1 package (12 ounces) egg tagliarini
1/2 pound sliced bacon, diced
1 pound chicken livers, sliced
1 cup chopped onions
1 cup sliced, fresh mushrooms
1/3 cup flour
1 can (10- ounces) chicken broth
1 full can water
1/2 cup burgundy wine
1/2 teaspoon thyme
1/2 teaspoon Worcestershire sauce
1/4 cup chopped parsley

Cook egg tagliarini according to package directions; drain. Fry bacon until brown. Stir in chicken livers, onions, and mushrooms; sauté. Add flour, broth, 1 full can water, wine, thyme, and Worcestershire sauce; simmer for 5 minutes. Add parsley and serve over egg tagliarini. Makes 6 (1-1/2 cup) servings.

FETTUCCINE RIVIERA

I tasted a dish like this on the Love Boat. The fettuccine was so delicious that I decided to include it in this cookbook.

> 1 package (12 ounces) medium egg noodles
> 4 tablespoons butter
> 1/4 pound boiled ham, cut into strips
> 1 cup cooked chicken or turkey, cut into strips
> 1/4 pound mushrooms, sliced
> 1/2 pint (1 cup) half and half
> 4 egg yolks
> 1/2 cup grated Parmesan cheese
> Salt and pepper

Cook noodles according to package directions; drain. Melt butter and sauté ham, chicken, and mushrooms. Blend half and half with egg yolks. Pour over sautéed ingredients and bring to boil. Remove from heat. Add cooked noodles, grated cheese, and salt and pepper to taste. Toss together in pan. Makes 4 (2 cup) servings.

CHICKEN STROGANOFF

This recipe is a lighter version of stroganoff made with chicken.

> 1 clove garlic, minced
> 1/4 cup butter
> 2 tablespoons oil
> 2-1/2 to 3 pounds chicken, cut up
> 1/3 cup flour
> 1 teaspoon salt
> 1/4 teaspoon pepper
> 1 can (14-1/2 ounces) chicken broth
> 2 tablespoons flour
> 1 tablespoon minced dry onions
> 2 cups sliced mushrooms
> 1 cup sour cream
> 1 package (12 ounces) twistee egg noodles

Sauté garlic in butter and oil. Dredge chicken with flour, salt, and pepper; brown in butter. Combine broth with 2 tablespoons flour. Add broth, onions, and mushrooms to chicken. Simmer, covered, 30 minutes. Remove chicken from pan. Remove sauce from heat and cool slightly; whisk in sour cream. Cook twistee noodles according to package directions; drain. Top noodles with chicken and sauce. Makes 5 servings.

CHICKEN MARSALA

This chicken dish with a light tomato, wine, and herb sauce is perfect for a family dinner.

1/4 cup olive oil
2-1/2 pounds chicken parts
1/4 cup chopped onion
1 teaspoon minced garlic
1/2 cup Florio Dry Marsala wine
1 can (15 ounces) marinara sauce
1 can (16 ounces) whole peeled tomatoes, cut up
1/4 teaspoon pepper
1 tablespoon chopped parsley
1/2 teaspoon sweet basil leaves
1 package (12 ounces) medium egg noodles
Grated Parmesan cheese

Heat olive oil in Dutch oven or large saucepot. Brown chicken on all sides. Add onion and garlic; cook until soft. Add wine. Simmer, uncovered, 10 minutes. Add marinara sauce, tomatoes, pepper, parsley, and basil; continue simmering about 25 minutes, stirring occasionally. Cook noodles according to package directions; drain. Serve sauce and chicken over noodles. Sprinkle with Parmesan cheese. Makes 4 servings.

EASY CLAM LINGUINE

Three of my brothers really like clam pasta dishes but each one in different ways. I thought you might be interested in all three variations. My brother Paskey loves this recipe.

> **2 teaspoons minced garlic**
> **3 tablespoons chopped green onion (white portion only)**
> **2 tablespoons butter**
> **2 tablespoons olive oil**
> **1/2 cup chopped parsley**
> **2 cans (6-1/2 ounces each) chopped clams with juice**
> **1/2 package (8 ounces) linguine**
> **Grated Parmesan cheese (optional)**

In a 3-quart saucepan, sauté garlic and green onion in butter and olive oil for 5 minutes. Add parsley and clams to garlic and onion mixture; simmer another 5 minutes. Cook linguine according to package directions; drain. Toss with clam mixture and serve. Sprinkle with Parmesan cheese, if desired. Makes 4 (1 cup) servings.

CLAM SAUCE AND TENDERTHIN LONG NOODLES

My brother Vincent likes this clam pasta dish. This is the way his wife, Mildred, makes it. The touch of lemon in the recipe changes the original sauce.

2 cans (10 ounces each) whole baby clams
1 cup chopped onion
3 cloves garlic, minced
1/3 cup olive oil
1/4 cup butter
1 teaspoon oregano
1/2 teaspoon salt
1/8 teaspoon fresh ground pepper
1 package (12 ounces) tenderthin long noodles
1/4 cup chopped parsley
1 tablespoon lemon juice
1 teaspoon grated lemon rind

Drain and reserve juice from clams. In a 10-inch frying pan sauté onion and garlic in olive oil and butter. Add clam juice, oregano, salt, and pepper and bring to boil over high heat. Cook until reduced to 1-1/2 cups, about 5 minutes. Cook tenderthin noodles according to package directions; drain. Add clams, parsley, lemon juice, and lemon rind to sauce. Heat thoroughly and serve over noodles. Makes 6 (1-1/2 cup) servings.

RED CLAM LINGUINE

My brother Tom likes the touch of red in his clam sauce.

> 1/2 package (8 ounces) linguine
> 3 cloves garlic, minced
> 1/4 cup butter
> 1 can (10 ounces) whole baby clams or
>   2 cans (6-1/2 ounces each) chopped clams
> 1 can (7-3/4 ounces) marinara sauce
> 2 tablespoons chopped parsley
> Grated Parmesan cheese (optional)

Cook linguine according to package directions; drain. In saucepan, combine garlic, butter, clams with juice, and marinara sauce. Bring to boil, reduce heat, and simmer 5 minutes. Stir in parsley. Serve over linguine and sprinkle with Parmesan cheese, if desired. Makes 3 (1-1/4 cup) servings.

VERMICELLI WITH WHITE CLAM SAUCE

My son-in-law John loves the touch of basil and thyme in his clam dish.

1 package (16 ounces) vermicelli
1/2 cup butter
2 teaspoons olive oil
1-1/2 tablespoons minced garlic
1/2 teaspoon basil
1/4 teaspoon thyme
1/2 teaspoon fresh ground pepper
2 cans (6-1/2 ounces each) chopped clams with juice
3 teaspoons chopped parsley
Grated Parmesan cheese (optional)

Cook vermicelli according to package directions; drain. Melt butter in saucepan with olive oil over medium-low heat. Add garlic and sauté for 2 to 3 minutes. Do not let the garlic brown or burn. Add the basil, thyme, and pepper; simmer 1 to 2 minutes. Add clams and bring to slow boil for 2 to 3 minutes. Remove from heat, stir in parsley, and serve over vermicelli. Top with Parmesan cheese, if desired. Makes 4 servings (2 cups each).

EGG TAGLIARINI WITH SOUR CREAM CLAM SAUCE

My nephew Dennis contributed this dish to my first cooking school, and it has been a favorite ever since. You will find this dish simple to make and so delightful.

2 cans (10 ounces each) whole baby clams
1 package (12 ounces) egg tagliarini
2-3 cloves garlic, minced
1 cup butter, cut up
1 cup sour cream (room temperature)
1/4 cup chopped parsley

Drain clams, reserving 1 tablespoon clam liquid. Pour remaining liquid into pasta water. Cook egg tagliarini according to package directions; drain. In saucepan, sauté garlic in 2 tablespoons butter. Add remaining butter and heat until melted. Add clams and reserved clam liquid. Heat but do not boil. Remove from heat and stir in sour cream and parsley. Top egg tagliarini with sauce. Makes 6 (1-1/4 cup) servings.

CRAB VERMICELLI

This dish is so expensive in restaurants and so easy for you to do at home. All you need with it is a tossed green salad. The recipe is also delicious with 1 pound of shrimp instead of crab.

2 to 3 cloves garlic, minced
1 cup butter
1/4 cup sliced green onion tops
3/4 teaspoon oregano
1/4 teaspoon salt
3/4 cup sauterne wine
1 pound crabmeat, cooked
4 tablespoons chopped parsley
8 ounces vermicelli
Juice of 1/2 lemon

In a 10-inch frying pan, sauté garlic in melted butter. Stir in green onion tops, oregano, salt, and wine and simmer 2 minutes. Add crabmeat and parsley. Cook vermicelli according to package directions; drain. In pan, toss vermicelli with crab mixture. Sprinkle with lemon juice. Makes 4 (2 cup) servings.

MAMA'S CRAB CIOPPINO

Crab cioppino is one of Mama's most famous recipes. Made with uncooked crab, this dish is exceptional.

3 cloves garlic, minced
3/4 cup to 1 cup olive oil, minimum
2 crabs, live, cracked and cleaned
1 cup chopped, fresh parsley
3 cans (15 ounces each) marinara sauce
2 cans (6 ounces each) tomato paste
1 cup water
Salt and pepper
1 package (16 ounces) vermicelli

Sauté garlic in olive oil. Add crab and sauté till crabs are red, stirring occasionally. Add parsley, marinara sauce, tomato paste, and water. Heat to boiling and simmer 5 to 10 minutes. Salt and pepper to taste. While sauce is simmering, cook vermicelli according to package directions; drain. Top vermicelli with sauce and crab. Makes 6 servings.

CRAB CIOPPINO SPAGHETTI

Mama's version of this classic includes cooked crabmeat.

1-1/2 cups chopped onion
1 cup chopped green pepper
2 cloves garlic, minced
2 tablespoons olive oil
2 cans (15 ounces each) marinara sauce
1/4 cup burgundy wine
1/2 teaspoon salt
1/4 teaspoon pepper
1 pound cooked crabmeat
1 package (16 ounces) spaghetti

Sauté onion, green pepper, and garlic in olive oil. Add marinara sauce, wine, salt, and pepper; simmer 10 minutes. Add crab and heat through. Prepare spaghetti according to package directions; drain. Serve sauce over spaghetti. Makes 6 (2 cup) servings.

ARTICHOKE CRAB SAUTÉ WITH EGG TAGLIARINI

This seafood recipe is an elegant, easy dish to make.

1 package (12 ounces) egg tagliarini
1 can (15 ounces) marinara sauce
2 jars (6 ounces each) marinated artichoke hearts,
**   drained**
1 pound cooked crabmeat
6 tablespoons butter
1/4 cup grated Parmesan cheese

Cook egg tagliarini according to package directions; drain. Heat marinara sauce. Sauté artichokes and crab in butter until heated. On serving platter, layer egg tagliarini, marinara sauce, and crab mixture. Garnish with Parmesan cheese. Makes 6 (1-1/3 cup) servings.

SCALLOP FETTUCCINE

My niece Donna loves fettuccine dishes. This recipe of hers is sensational especially when fresh asparagus is in season.

1 package (10 ounces) fettuccine
1 pound asparagus, cut diagonally into 1-inch pieces
2 tablespoons salt
1 pound scallops
3 lemon wedges
1 cup whipping cream
4 teaspoons grated lemon peel
1/2 teaspoon salt
2 tablespoons butter, softened
2 tablespoons grated Parmesan cheese
2 tablespoons chopped parsley, preferably Italian

Cook fettuccine and asparagus in 5 quarts rapidly boiling, salted water for 8 minutes. Add scallops and lemon wedges; cook another 5 minutes. Heat cream in a 10-inch frying pan over medium-high heat until bubbling. Add lemon peel and salt; boil for 30 seconds. Reduce heat to low and add drained fettuccine, asparagus, scallops (remove lemon wedges), butter, Parmesan cheese, and parsley. Toss until fettuccine is evenly coated. Makes 4 (2 cup) servings.

ANCHOVIES WITH SPAGHETTINI

Don't let the anchovies scare you away from this dish. The anchovies are mashed to blend in the sauce so this dish is not fishy.

> 1 package (12 ounces) egg spaghettini
> 2 medium cloves garlic, minced
> 1/3 cup olive oil
> 1 can (2 ounces) anchovies
> 3 tablespoons chopped parsley
> 2 ounces (approximately 16 to 18) black Greek olives, pitted and sliced
> 1/2 teaspoon crushed red pepper
> 1/4 teaspoon oregano
> Grated Parmesan cheese

Cook egg spaghettini according to package directions; drain. Sauté garlic in olive oil for 1 minute. Add remaining ingredients, except Parmesan cheese, and sauté on medium-low heat for 3 minutes, mashing anchovies until blended. Toss with spaghettini until oil is almost absorbed. Sprinkle with Parmesan cheese. Makes 6 (1 cup) servings.

CLASSIC TUNA AND NOODLES

This recipe is a fast, easy, old-time favorite.

1/2 package (6 ounces) medium egg noodles
1 can (10-3/4 ounces) cream of mushroom soup
1 cup milk
1 can (6-1/2 ounces) tuna, drained
1 cup grated Cheddar cheese
1 can (2-1/2 ounces) sliced mushrooms
1/2 cup sliced, stuffed green olives
1/2 cup crushed potato chips

Cook noodles according to package directions; drain. In saucepan, combine soup, milk, and tuna; bring to boil. Stir in cooked noodles, cheese, mushrooms, and olives. Pour into buttered 1-1/2-quart casserole dish. Top with potato chips. Bake at 375°F for 15 to 20 minutes. Makes 6 (1 cup) servings.

PRAWNS GNOCCHI

Gnocchi is a new pasta shape, which is great with seafood.

> **1/2 package (6 ounces) gnocchi**
> **6 tablespoons butter**
> **2 tablespoons flour**
> **1-1/2 cups half and half**
> **1/4 teaspoon salt**
> **1/8 teaspoon white pepper**
> **1/4 cup sauterne wine**
> **1 jar (2 ounces) sliced pimientos**
> **1/2 cup sliced green onions**
> **1/4 pound mushrooms, sliced**
> **1/2 cup thinly sliced green pepper, 1 inch long**
> **1 teaspoon minced garlic**
> **1/2 pound raw jumbo prawns, cut lengthwise**
>   **and crosswise**
> **1 tablespoon lemon juice (optional)**
> **1/4 cup chopped parsley**

Cook gnocchi according to package directions; drain. Melt 2 tablespoons butter on low heat in heavy saucepan. Remove from heat and whisk in flour. Return to low heat and cook approximately 1 to 2 minutes, stirring constantly. Remove from heat and stir in half and half, salt, and pepper. Return to medium heat, stirring constantly, until sauce thickens slightly. Stir in wine and pimientos and remove from heat.

In frying pan sauté green onions, mushrooms, green pepper, and garlic in 4 tablespoons butter for 2 minutes. Add prawns and sauté 2 minutes. Add sauce and lemon juice and simmer, covered, for 5 minutes. Stir in parsley and serve over gnocchi. Makes 5 (1 cup) servings.

RED PEPPER AND SHRIMP PASTA

That touch of red pepper makes this dish delightful.

> 2 cloves garlic, minced
> 1/3 cup olive oil
> 1/2 teaspoon crushed red pepper
> 1-2 drops red pepper sauce
> 1/2 package (6 ounces) egg spaghettini
> 1/2 pound shrimp, cleaned and deveined
> 1 lemon, thinly sliced
> 1/4 cup grated Parmesan cheese
> 2 tablespoons chopped parsley
> Grated Parmesan cheese

Over low heat sauté garlic in olive oil; add red pepper and red pepper sauce. Set aside. Cook egg spaghettini according to package directions. During the last 3 minutes of cooking, add shrimp and lemon slices; drain. Toss pasta with sauce, Parmesan cheese, and parsley. Sprinkle with additional Parmesan cheese. Makes 4 (1 cup) servings.

SALMON SPAGHETTI

For people who don't like crab or shrimp, try this dish.

2 medium cloves garlic, minced
1 cup butter
1/4 cup sliced green onion tops
3/4 teaspoon oregano
3/4 cup sauterne wine
1 can (15-1/2 ounces) sockeye salmon, drained
4 tablespoons chopped parsley
8 ounces thin spaghetti
Juice of 1/2 lemon

In a 10-inch frying pan, sauté garlic in melted butter. Stir in green onion tops and oregano; simmer 2 minutes. Add wine and simmer another 2 minutes. Add salmon and parsley and heat. Cook thin spaghetti according to package directions; drain. In pan, toss spaghetti with salmon mixture until sauce is slightly absorbed. Sprinkle with lemon juice. Makes 5 (1 cup) servings.

SALMON FETTUCCINE

The abundance of salmon in Alaska inspired my niece Marla and her husband, Dale, to create this fabulous fettuccine dish.

6 cloves garlic, minced
2 tablespoons olive oil
1 pound fresh salmon fillets, cut in small strips
3/4 cup sauterne wine
Salt
Freshly ground pepper
8 ounces fettuccine
8 ounces spinach fettuccine
1-1/4 cup whipping cream
2 cups Parmesan cheese
3 tablespoons chopped parsley

In a large frying pan, sauté garlic in olive oil. Add salmon and wine; salt and pepper to taste. Poach the salmon, covered, in wine and garlic for 7 to 8 minutes, or until fish flakes with a fork.

Cook fettuccine and spinach fettuccine according to package directions. Just before pasta is cooked, add whipping cream to salmon and cook 2 to 3 minutes to blend flavors. Drain pasta and return to pot. Add salmon sauce and Parmesan cheese and toss together until cheese melts. Serve on platter and sprinkle with parsley. Makes 4 (2-1/4 cup) servings.

ELEGANT STUFF-A-RONI

Stuff-a-roni, commonly known as manicotti, is a great company dish.

White Sauce
>1/2 cup butter
>1/2 cup flour
>1 cup milk
>2 cans (14-1/2 ounces each) chicken broth
>Salt
>Dash white pepper
>1/2 cup Green Hungarian wine

In heavy saucepan, melt butter. Remove from heat and whisk in flour. Return to low heat and cook approximately 3 minutes, stirring constantly. Remove from heat and stir in milk, chicken broth, salt, and pepper. Return to medium heat, stirring constantly until sauce comes to boil. Stir in wine.

Filling
>1-1/2 cups finely chopped, cooked turkey or chicken
>5 ounces Gruyere or Swiss cheese, grated
>1/2 cup white sauce (recipe above)
>1/4 cup Green Hungarian wine
>1 egg, beaten
>1 tablespoon minced parsley
>1 package (3-3/4 ounces) manicotti
>Grated Parmesan cheese
>Chopped parsley for garnish

Combine turkey, Gruyere cheese, white sauce, wine, egg, and minced parsley. Fill uncooked manicotti according to package directions. Cover bottom of a 2-quart oblong baking dish with 1 cup of sauce. Arrange filled manicotti in a single layer in baking dish. Cover manicotti completely with remaining sauce. Cover dish tightly with foil and bake at 375°F, 1 hour. Garnish top with Parmesan cheese and parsley. Makes 4 servings, 2 each. (To prepare in advance, bake then refrigerate or freeze.)

PASTA STUFFED PARMA STYLE

I love serving this dish as a first course to a meal. When I make it, I prefer using ricotta cheese.

2 cans (15 ounces each) marinara sauce
Water (oven, 1/2 cup; microwave oven, 1-1/4 cups)
1-1/2 cups small curd cottage cheese or ricotta
1 egg, slightly beaten
1 tablespoon minced parsley
1/4 cup grated Parmesan cheese
1/2 teaspoon dried sweet basil leaves
1/2 teaspoon nutmeg
1/2 teaspoon salt
1/4 teaspoon pepper
1 package (3.75 ounces) manicotti

Heat marinara sauce with water. In bowl, combine remaining ingredients for filling. Fill manicotti as directed on package. Cover bottom of a 2-quart baking dish with 1 cup of marinara sauce. Arrange filled manicotti in single layer in baking dish. Cover completely with remaining sauce. Cover dish tightly with foil and bake at 375°F, 1 hour; or cover with plastic wrap and microwave on high for 6 minutes, then approximately 25 minutes on medium-low, turning occasionally. Makes 4 servings, 2 each. (To prepare in advance, bake then refrigerate or freeze.)

MANICOTTI FLORENTINE

This filling tastes like ravioli and is a perfect main course.

2 cans (15 ounces each) marinara sauce
Water (oven, 1/2 cup; microwave oven, 1-1/4 cups)
1/2 pound ground beef
1/4 cup minced onion
1/2 package frozen spinach, thawed
1/4 cup bread crumbs
1/4 cup grated Parmesan cheese
2 eggs, slightly beaten
1 teaspoon salt
1/4 teaspoon pepper
1 package (3.75 ounces) manicotti

Heat marinara sauce with water. Brown ground beef with onion; drain off excess fat. Blend together meat, spinach, and remaining ingredients. Fill manicotti as directed on package. Cover bottom of a 2-quart baking dish with 1 cup of marinara sauce. Arrange filled manicotti in single layer in baking dish. Cover completely with remaining sauce. Cover dish with foil and bake at 375°F, 1 hour; or cover tightly with plastic wrap and microwave on high for 6 minutes, and approximately 25 minutes on medium-low, turning occasionally. Makes 4 servings, 2 each. (To prepare in advance, bake then refrigerate or freeze.)

MONTEREY CHEESE AND CHICKEN MANICOTTI

Monterey Jack cheese makes this chicken and broccoli dish outstanding.

Cheese Sauce
> 1/2 cup butter
> 1/2 cup flour
> 3 cups chicken broth
> 1 cup milk
> 2 cups (10 ounces) grated fresh Monterey Jack cheese
> 1/4 teaspoon Tabasco sauce
> Salt and pepper

To make cheese sauce, melt butter in heavy saucepan. Remove from heat and whisk in flour. Return to low heat and cook approximately 3 minutes, stirring constantly. Remove from heat and stir in broth and milk. Return to medium heat, stirring constantly until sauce comes to a boil. Add remaining ingredients.

Filling
> 2 eggs, beaten
> 1 cup minced, cooked chicken
> 1/2 package (10 ounces) frozen, chopped broccoli,
>   thawed and drained
> 1/2 cup fresh bread crumbs
> 1/4 cup cheese sauce (recipe above)
> 1/3 cup grated dry Monterey Jack cheese
> 2 teaspoons finely chopped parsley
> 1 clove garlic, minced
> 1/2 teaspoon nutmeg
> Salt and pepper
> 1 package (3.75 ounces) manicotti

In bowl, combine filling ingredients; salt and pepper to taste. Fill manicotti with filling. Cover bottom of a 2-quart baking dish with 1 cup cheese sauce. Arrange filled manicotti in single layer in baking dish. Cover with remaining sauce. Cover dish tightly with foil and bake at 375°F, 1 hour. Makes 4 servings, 2 each. (To prepare in advance, bake then refrigerate or freeze.)

CRAB AND SHRIMP STUFFED MANICOTTI

This tantalizing dish is an outstanding combination of crab and shrimp in a delicate curry sauce.

White Sauce

6 tablespoons butter
1/2 teaspoon curry powder
6 tablespoons flour
1/2 teaspoon salt
1/4 teaspoon white pepper

1 can (14-1/2 ounces) chicken broth
3/4 cup milk
3/4 cup water
1/2 cup dry vermouth
   or dry white wine

In a heavy saucepan, melt butter and blend in curry powder. Remove from heat and whisk in flour. Return to low heat and cook approximately 2 minutes, stirring constantly. Remove from heat and stir in salt, pepper, chicken broth, milk, and water. Return to medium heat, stirring constantly, until sauce thickens. Stir in wine and remove from heat.

Filling

2 cups (12 ounces)
   coarsely chopped crabmeat
4 ounces mild Cheddar cheese,
   grated
1 egg, beaten
1 small clove garlic, minced

1 tablespoon lemon juice
2 tablespoons minced parsley
1/2 cup white sauce (recipe above)
1 package (3-3/4 ounces) manicotti
1 cup (4 ounces) baby shrimp

Combine crabmeat, cheese, egg, garlic, lemon juice, parsley, and 1/2 cup of white sauce. Fill uncooked manicotti according to package directions. Cover bottom of a 2-quart baking dish with 1 cup sauce. Arrange filled manicotti in single layer in baking dish. Add shrimp to remaining sauce and pour over top of manicotti. Cover dish tightly with foil and bake at 375°F, 1 hour. Makes 4 servings, 2 each. (To prepare in advance, bake then refrigerate or freeze.)

MANICOTTI PIZZA STYLE

For the pizza lover, here is a touch of pizza in a stuffed shell.

> 1/2 pound Italian sweet sausage
> 2 cans (15 ounces each) marinara sauce
> 1/2 cup water
> 1 cup (8 ounces) ricotta or cottage cheese
> 1/4 cup grated Parmesan cheese
> 1/2 cup grated Monterey Jack cheese
> 1 egg
> 1/4 cup chopped salami slices
> 2 tablespoons chopped green pepper
> 1 package (3-3/4 ounces) manicotti

Remove casings from sausage; brown. Add marinara sauce and water; heat to boil. Combine ricotta, Parmesan, Monterey Jack cheese, egg, salami, and green pepper. Fill uncooked manicotti with cheese mixture according to package directions. Cover bottom of a 2-quart baking dish with 1 cup sauce. Arrange filled manicotti in a single layer in baking dish. Top with remaining sauce. Cover dish tightly with foil; bake at 375°F, 1 hour. Makes 4 servings, 2 each. (To prepare in advance, bake then refrigerate or freeze.)

ZUCCHINI STUFF-A-RONI ALLA PANNA

This recipe is a great dish for vegetarians.

Sauce
4 tablespoons butter

5 tablespoons flour

1 cup hot milk

1 can (14-1/2 ounces)
   chicken broth

1 cup half and half

1/2 cup dry vermouth

2 dashes nutmeg

In saucepan, melt butter. Remove from heat and whisk in flour. Return to low heat and cook 2 minutes, stirring constantly. Add hot milk and chicken broth, stirring constantly, until thickened. Remove from heat and slowly stir in half and half, vermouth, and nutmeg. Bring to a boil.

Filling
1/2 cup chopped onion

2 tablespoons butter

1 pound zucchini, shredded

3/4 teaspoon salt

3 tablespoons chopped parsley

3/4 cup Parmesan Cheese

2 eggs

2 dashes pepper

1 package (3-3/4 ounces)
   manicotti

2 dashes nutmeg (optional)

Sauté onion in melted butter. Sprinkle 1/4 teaspoon salt on coarsely shredded zucchini and drain in colander for 30 minutes. Rinse well and squeeze zucchini tightly in thin cloth towel until dry. Mix together onion, zucchini, parsley, cheese, eggs, 1/2 teaspoon salt, and pepper. Fill manicotti according to package directions. Set aside.

Cover bottom of a 2-quart, oblong baking dish with 1 cup sauce. Arrange filled manicotti in a single layer in baking dish. Cover manicotti completely with remaining sauce. Cover dish tightly with foil and bake at 375°F, 1 hour; or cover with plastic wrap and microwave on high for 6 minutes and approximately 25 minutes on medium-low, turning occasionally. Garnish with additional Parmesan cheese and nutmeg, if desired. Makes 4 servings, 2 each. (To prepare in advance, bake then refrigerate or freeze.)

CHICKEN STUFF-A-RONI WITH CHEESE

The Cheddar cheese must be sharp to get the ultimate flavor of this stuff-a-roni dish.

Filling
1-1/2 cups finely chopped, cooked chicken, turkey, or
    tuna
1/2 cup finely chopped onion
1/4 cup minced parsley
1/4 teaspoon ground thyme
1/4 teaspoon garlic salt
1/2 cup finely chopped celery
1 cup grated, sharp Cheddar cheese
1/4 cup dry vermouth or dry white wine
Salt and pepper

In bowl, combine filling ingredients; salt and pepper to taste.

Sauce

1/2 cup butter	2 cups grated, sharp Cheddar cheese
1/2 cup flour	1/4 teaspoon Tabasco
3 cups chicken broth	Salt and pepper
1 cup milk	1 package (3-3/4 ounces) manicotti

In saucepan, melt butter. Remove from heat and whisk in flour. Stir in broth and milk; cook until thickened, stirring frequently. Add remaining sauce ingredients. Fill manicotti as directed on package. Cover bottom of a 2-quart baking dish with 1 cup cheese sauce. Arrange filled manicotti in single layer in baking dish. Completely cover with remaining sauce. Cover dish tightly with foil and bake at 375°F, 1 hour; or cover with plastic wrap and microwave on high for 6 minutes, then approximately 25 minutes on medium-low, turning occasionally. Makes 4 (2 each) servings. (To prepare in advance, bake then refrigerate or freeze.)

FROM THE OVEN

MOUSSAKA LASAGNA

This recipe is an Italian version of a famous Greek dish.

2 tablespoons butter	1 eggplant (approximately 1-1/4
2 tablespoons oil	pounds), sliced 1/4 inch thick

Melt 2 tablespoons butter with oil in flat baking pan. Coat eggplant on each side with butter/oil mixture; single layer. Bake at 400°F, 10 minutes on each side.

Meat Sauce

1/2 pound ground lamb or beef	1/2 teaspoon salt
2 cans (15 ounces each)	1/4 teaspoon pepper
marinara sauce	2 dashes cinnamon
1/2 cup dry vermouth or	1 package (8 ounces) wide lasagna
white wine	12 ounces Monterey Jack cheese,
1/2 cup water	sliced

Brown meat; drain. Stir in marinara sauce, wine, water, salt, pepper, and cinnamon; bring to a boil. Layer meat sauce, uncooked lasagna, eggplant, and cheese in a 3-quart oblong baking dish. Repeat layers, ending with lasagna and sauce. Cover tightly with foil. Bake at 375°F, 45 minutes. While lasagna is baking, prepare the white sauce.

White Sauce

3 tablespoons butter	1/2 teaspoon salt
3 tablespoons flour	2 eggs, beaten
1-1/4 cups milk	

Melt butter in saucepan. Remove from heat; whisk in flour. Return to low heat and cook 3 minutes, stirring constantly. Whisk in milk and salt. Cook, stirring constantly, until thick. Remove from heat; whisk in eggs. Pour white sauce evenly over baked lasagna and return to oven. Bake at 450°F, 15 minutes. Let stand 10 minutes before cutting. Makes 8 to 10 servings. (To prepare in advance, bake then refrigerate or freeze.)

KATHERINE'S EASY SPINACH LASAGNA

Once you've tried this recipe, you'll never make lasagna the old-fashioned way of cooking it first. The pasta, cooking in the sauce, makes this dish outstanding.

Meat Sauce
1/2 pound lean ground beef
2 cans (15 ounces each) marinara sauce
1/2 cup dry vermouth
1/2 cup water
Pinch cinnamon (optional)
Salt

Brown meat and drain off excess fat. Add marinara sauce, wine, water, cinnamon, and salt to taste. Bring to boil.

Spinach Filling
1 package (10 ounces) frozen chopped spinach, thawed
1 cup (8 ounces) ricotta cheese
1/2 cup grated, dry Monterey Jack or Parmesan cheese
2 eggs
1/2 teaspoon salt
1/4 teaspoon pepper
1/8 teaspoon nutmeg

Squeeze all liquid from spinach. Combine all ingredients for spinach filling in food processor or blender. Blend until smooth.

Remaining Ingredients
1 package (8 ounces) wide lasagna
12 ounces mozzarella or Monterey Jack cheese, sliced
Grated, dry Monterey Jack or Parmesan cheese
    (optional)

In a 3-quart baking dish, layer meat sauce, uncooked lasagna, sliced cheese, meat sauce, and lasagna. Spread spinach filling, small amount of sauce, sliced cheese, lasagna, and sauce. Cover dish tightly with foil and bake at 375°F, 1 hour; or cover dish with plastic wrap and microwave on high for 8 minutes and approximately 30 minutes on medium-low, turning once. Garnish top with dry Monterey Jack cheese, if desired. Makes 8 servings. (To prepare in advance, bake then refrigerate or freeze.)

LASAGNA ROLLUPS

I call this my "Pasta—with a Flair" recipe. This lasagna dish is so elegant to serve and freezes beautifully.

6 strips extra wide lasagna

Cook lasagna according to package directions for 10 minutes. Drain and rinse in cold water.

White Sauce Filling

2 tablespoons butter	3 egg yolks, slightly beaten
2 tablespoons flour	8 ounces mozzarella cheese, grated
1-1/2 cups hot milk	1/8 pound prosciutto, mortadella,
Dash pepper	or ham, diced

In saucepan, melt butter. Remove from heat and whisk in flour. Return to low heat and cook approximately 3 minutes, stirring constantly. Remove from heat and stir in hot milk and pepper. Return to medium heat, stirring constantly until all sauce thickens and boils for 1 minute. Remove from heat and quickly whisk in egg yolks. Stir in cheese, then prosciutto.

Meat Sauce

1/4 pound ground beef	1/4 cup dry vermouth
1 can (15 ounces) marinara sauce	1/4 teaspoon salt

Brown ground beef; drain. Add marinara sauce, wine, and salt. Bring to boil.

Topping

2 tablespoons butter	2 tablespoons Florio Dry Marsala wine
1/4 pound sliced mushrooms	
1/8 pound (1/4 cup) prosciutto, mortadella, or ham, diced	1/8 teaspoon freshly ground pepper

In frying pan, sauté mushrooms in butter for 3 minutes. Add prosciutto, wine, and pepper and simmer 2 minutes.

To assemble, cut extra wide lasagna strips in half, crosswise. Spread each half with white sauce and roll. Place in a 2-quart baking dish, seam-side down. Pour meat sauce over rollups, then topping. Bake, uncovered, at 375°F, 20 minutes. Makes 6 servings (2 rolls each).

EASY OVEN LASAGNA

This is an easy dish to prepare because you don't have to cook the lasagna first.

1/2 pound ground beef
3/4 cup water
2 cans (15 ounces each) marinara sauce
1 teaspoon salt
1 package (8 ounces) lasagna, uncooked
1 cup ricotta or small curd cottage cheese
12 ounces mozzarella or Monterey Jack cheese,
    sliced or grated
1/4 cup grated Parmesan cheese

Brown ground beef; drain. Add water, marinara sauce, and salt; bring to a boil. In a 2-quart baking dish, layer marinara sauce, uncooked lasagna, and ricotta and mozzarella cheese; repeat layers, ending with sauce. Cover dish tightly with foil and bake at 375°F, 1 hour. In a microwave oven, cover baking dish tightly with plastic wrap; microwave on high for 8 minutes, then about 30 minutes on medium-low, turning occasionally. Let stand 10 minutes before cutting. Garnish with Parmesan cheese. Makes 6 servings. (To prepare in advance, bake then refrigerate or freeze.)

BAKED FETTUCCINE

Although baking fettuccine is unusual, this recipe is an enjoyable dish.

1 package (12 ounces) fettuccine
1 package (10 ounces) frozen peas, thawed
3 egg yolks, beaten
1-1/2 cups half and half
3/4 cup butter, melted
3/4 cup grated Parmesan cheese
1-1/2 tablespoons parsley flakes
1-1/2 teaspoons dried sweet basil leaves, crushed
1-1/2 teaspoons onion powder
1/2 teaspoon salt
1/8 teaspoon pepper

Cook fettuccine according to package directions; drain. Add peas to fettuccine and set aside. Combine egg yolks, half and half, butter, cheese, parsley, basil, onion powder, salt, and pepper. Stir until well mixed and toss with fettuccine. Pour into a 3-quart, shallow baking dish. Cover tightly with greased foil. Bake at 400°F, 20 minutes. Makes 8 servings.

BOW TIE RAVIOLI

Children love the butterfly shape in this ravioli recipe.

2 cans (15 ounces each) marinara sauce
1 can (16 ounces) whole tomatoes, cut up
1/4 cup Florio Dry Marsala wine
1 teaspoon salt
3/4 teaspoon pepper
2 tablespoons olive oil
1/2 pound ground beef
1 medium onion, sliced
1 package (10 ounces) frozen, chopped spinach,
    thawed
1 clove garlic, minced
1 cup grated Parmesan cheese
1/4 teaspoon nutmeg
1 package (10 ounces) bow ties

Combine marinara sauce, tomatoes, wine, 1/2 teaspoon salt and 1/2 teaspoon pepper. Heat to boiling and simmer 10 minutes. In hot olive.oil, brown meat with onions. Squeeze excess liquid from spinach; add to meat and cook 2 minutes. Add garlic, 3/4 cup Parmesan cheese, nutmeg, 1/2 teaspoon salt and 1/4 teaspoon pepper. Blend in food processor or blender until well mixed.

Cook bow ties according to package directions; drain and rinse in cold water. In a 3-quart baking dish, layer sauce, bow ties, sauce, meat mixture, sauce, bow ties, and sauce. Top with 1/4 cup Parmesan cheese. Bake at 350°F, 30 minutes. Makes 8 servings.

CHICKEN CACCIATORE WITH ARTICHOKE HEARTS

This chicken cacciatore dish is a great entertaining recipe. It was given to me by my sister-in-law Mildred. She is a very talented San Francisco Peninsula hostess, who can cook gourmet meals for 2 to 50 people with ease.

1 jar marinated artichoke hearts
2 tablespoons olive oil
1 frying chicken (3-1/2 pounds), cut up
Flour
2 cloves garlic, minced
1 can (28 ounces) tomatoes, cut up
1-1/4 teaspoons salt
1/2 teaspoon oregano
1/2 teaspoon dried sweet basil leaves
1/2 teaspoon pepper
1/2 pound mushrooms, sliced
1/2 cup dry sherry
1 package (16 ounces) cut macaroni

Drain liquid from artichoke hearts into large skillet; add olive oil and heat. Dredge chicken with flour and brown in oil mixture. Remove chicken from oil and place in large casserole. In skillet sauté garlic 2 to 3 minutes. Add artichoke hearts, tomatoes, salt, oregano, basil, pepper, and mushrooms. When heated and thoroughly mixed, pour over chicken. Cover and bake at 350°F, 1 hour. Add sherry; stir and return to oven for 10 minutes.

Cook cut macaroni according to package directions; drain. Toss with sauce and serve with chicken. Makes 4 servings.

BAKED GNOCCHI PARMESAN

You can make this delicious pasta accompaniment ahead of time.

1 package (12 ounces) gnocchi
6 tablespoons butter
3 tablespoons flour
3 cups milk
1/2 teaspoon salt
1/8 teaspoon grated nutmeg
3/4 cup grated Parmesan cheese

Cook gnocchi according to package directions; drain. Melt butter in saucepan and stir in flour. Cook over medium heat, stirring constantly, 2 minutes. Slowly stir in milk, salt, and nutmeg. Cook, stirring constantly, until mixture just comes to a boil. Remove from heat; stir in 1/4 cup Parmesan cheese. Pour 1 cup sauce into bottom of a 2-quart, shallow baking dish. Pour in cooked gnocchi and top with remaining sauce. Sprinkle 1/2 cup Parmesan cheese over top. Bake at 400°F for 10-15 minutes or until top is golden brown and crusty. Makes 7 (1 cup) servings.

CHICKEN TETRAZZINI

This recipe gives you a great way to use leftover chicken or turkey, besides being so easy to make.

1/2 pound mushrooms, sliced
1 small green pepper, slivered
1/4 cup butter
3 tablespoons flour
1/2 cup chicken broth
1 pint whipping cream
1/2 teaspoon salt
1/4 teaspoon pepper
2-1/2 cups diced, cooked chicken
3 tablespoons chopped pimientos
1/4 cup sherry
2 egg yolks, beaten
12 ounces spaghetti, cooked
1/2 cup grated Parmesan cheese

Cook mushrooms and green pepper in butter for 5 minutes; remove from heat and blend in flour. Return to heat and add chicken broth, whipping cream, salt, and pepper, stirring constantly until sauce comes to a boil; boil 2 minutes. Stir in chicken, pimientos, and sherry; heat. Add a small amount of chicken mixture to egg yolks; stir egg yolks into remaining mixture.

Cook spaghetti according to package directions; drain. Toss chicken mixture with spaghetti in a 2-quart broilerproof casserole. Top with Parmesan cheese. Broil for 5 minutes, 4 inches from broiler, to brown lightly. Makes 4 (2 cup) servings.

SHELLS AND VEGETABLES GRATINATE

Don't be alarmed if the cheese smells while this dish is baking. The taste is delicious.

> 3 hot Italian sausages
> 2 cans (15 ounces each) marinara sauce
> 1/2 teaspoon salt
> 1/4 teaspoon pepper
> 1 package (12 ounces) large shells
> 1/2 pound mushrooms, sliced
> 1 large green pepper, sliced
> 3 zucchini, sliced
> 1 pound fontina cheese, sliced

Remove casings from sausage and brown in saucepan; drain. Add marinara sauce, salt, and pepper; bring to boil. Remove from heat. Cook large shells in 5 quarts of boiling, salted water for 11 minutes. Add mushrooms, pepper, and zucchini to pot; return to boil and cook 2 minutes. Drain and rinse in cold water.

In a 3-quart casserole dish, layer sauce, shell mixture, cheese; repeat layers, topping with cheese. Bake, uncovered, at 375°F, 30 minutes. Makes 6 servings.

LASAGNA AL FORNO

This recipe brings back the old-fashioned way of making lasagna by cooking the pasta first.

> 1/2 cup chopped onion
> 1 clove garlic, minced
> 2 tablespoons olive oil
> 1 pound ground beef
> 2 cans (15 ounces each) marinara sauce
> 1 teaspoon salt
> 1/4 teaspoon pepper
> 1 package (8 ounces) lasagna
> 1 pound mozzarella or Monterey Jack cheese,
>   sliced thin
> 4 hard cooked eggs, sliced
> 1/4 cup grated Parmesan cheese

Sauté onion and garlic in olive oil; add ground beef and brown. Drain off excess fat. Stir in marinara sauce, salt, and pepper; simmer 15 minutes. Cook lasagna as directed on package. In a 2-quart baking dish, layer sauce, lasagna, sliced cheese, eggs, and Parmesan cheese. Repeat layers; top with sauce and cheese. Bake, uncovered, at 400°F, 20 minutes; or cover tightly with plastic wrap and microwave about 6 minutes on high, then 11 minutes on medium-low, turning occasionally. Let stand 10 minutes. Makes 6 servings.

CHICKEN LASAGNA WITH VEGETABLES

Chicken lasagna is a delightful company dish, made with a white sauce and topped with a red sauce.

1 package (8 ounces) lasagna

Cook lasagna as directed on package for 10 minutes. Drain and rinse in cold water.

Mushroom Sauce

2 cans (10-1/2 ounces each) cream of mushroom soup
1 tablespoon instant minced onion
1 cup chicken broth
1/2 cup dry vermouth or dry white wine
Salt and pepper

In saucepan combine mushroom soup, onion, chicken broth, vermouth, and salt and pepper to taste; bring to boil.

Chicken Filling

3 cups cooked, diced chicken, turkey, or ham
1 package (10 ounces) frozen, chopped broccoli or spinach, thawed
1 cup grated mozzarella cheese
1/4 cup grated Parmesan cheese

Combine chicken, broccoli, mozzarella, and Parmesan cheese.

Tomato Sauce

1 can (7-3/4 ounces) marinara sauce
1/4 teaspoon dried orange peel (optional)

Mix marinara sauce and orange peel. In a 3-quart baking dish, layer mushroom sauce, lasagna, marinara and chicken filling. Repeat layers. Top with tomato sauce. Bake at 400°F, 30 minutes; or cover tightly with plastic wrap and microwave 6 minutes on high, then 11 minutes on medium-low, turning occasionally. Let stand 10 minutes. Makes 6 servings.

LASAGNA IMBOTTITO WITH MEATBALLS

Every Easter Mama made her lasagna with hard-cooked eggs as a special treat.

Sauce

1/2 cup chopped onion
1 clove garlic, minced
2 tablespoons olive oil
1 can (28 ounces) tomatoes
1 can (6 ounces) tomato paste
1/2 cup water

1 tablespoon minced parsley
2 teaspoons dried sweet basil
    leaves or oregano
1 teaspoon salt
1/4 teaspoon pepper

Sauté onion and garlic in olive oil. Add tomatoes, tomato paste, water, parsley, basil, salt, and pepper.

Meatballs

1 pound ground beef or pork
1/4 cup bread crumbs
1/4 cup grated Parmesan cheese
2 tablespoons minced parsley
1 egg, slightly beaten

2 tablespoons milk
1 teaspoon salt
1/4 teaspoon pepper
2 tablespoons oil

Combine meat, breat crumbs, Parmesan cheese, parsley, egg, milk, salt, and pepper; mix thoroughly. Shape into tiny meatballs and brown in frying pan with oil. Add to sauce and simmer 30 minutes.

1 package (8 ounces) lasagna
1 pound mozzarella or Monterey
    Jack Cheese, sliced thin

4 hard-cooked eggs, sliced
1 cup (8 ounces) ricotta or
    cottage cheese

Cook lasagna as directed on package. Drain and rinse in cold water. Place 1/2 cup sauce on bottom of a 2-quart baking dish. Layer lasagna, sauce with meatballs, mozzarella, eggs, and ricotta cheese. Repeat layers; end with sauce and top with grated Parmesan cheese. Bake, uncovered, at 400°F, 20 minutes; or cover tightly with plastic wrap and microwave for 6 minutes on high, then 11 minutes on medium-low, turning occasionally. Let stand 10 minutes. Makes 6 servings.

WON TON ROLLUPS

My son, Ralph, is married to a Japanese woman. His wife, Kako, loves Italian food and has developed this Japanese-Italian pasta dish for my book. Won Ton Rollups, Italian style, is a great two-culture cuisine combination.

6 strips extra wide lasagna

Cook lasagna according to package directions for 10 minutes. Drain and rinse in cold water. Pat dry with paper towels and cover with plastic wrap.

Filling

1 pound ground pork	2 teaspoons sugar
1/2 teaspoon salt	2 teaspoons soy sauce
2 teaspoons sesame oil	1 egg, beaten
1/2 cup finely chopped green onions	1 cup shredded mozzarella cheese
1 clove garlic, finely chopped	2 tablespoons dry sherry
1/2 cup finely chopped cabbage	1 tablespoon cornstarch
2 teaspoons fresh grated ginger	

Sauté ground pork with 1/4 teaspoon salt and 1 teaspoon sesame oil until cooked. Add green onions, garlic, cabbage, and ginger and simmer 4 minutes. Drain fat from sausage mixture in a strainer over a bowl for 10 minutes. Add sugar, 1/4 teaspoon salt, 1 teaspoon sesame oil, soy sauce, egg, mozzarella cheese, sherry, and cornstarch to sausage mixture and mix thoroughly. Let stand 20 minutes.

Brown Sauce

1 can (14-1/2 ounces) beef broth	3 tablespoons cornstarch
1/4 cup peanut oil	3/4 cup water
2 tablespoons soy sauce	Green onion tops, sliced (garnish)
3 tablespoons dry sherry	

Combine all ingredients with wire whisk. Bring to boil and simmer 5 minutes.

To assemble, cut extra wide lasagna strips in half, crosswise. Spread each half evenly with filling and roll. Place 1/2 cup of brown sauce in a 2-quart baking dish. Place rollups in baking dish, seam-side down. Pour remainder of brown sauce over rollups. Cover with foil and bake at 375°F, 20 minutes. Before serving, spoon sauce over rollups and garnish with sliced green onion tops. Makes 6 servings (2 rolls each).

BAKED EGGPLANT WITH MOSTACCIOLI

This delicious Sicilian dish is excellent with fresh ripe tomatoes.

1 eggplant (about 1-1/4 pounds)
Salt
Flour
Olive oil for frying
1/4 pound sliced bacon, cut in small pieces
1-1/2 cups chopped onions
4 cloves garlic, minced
4 tablespoons olive oil
2 pounds ripe tomatoes, peeled and diced
1 small red pepper, slivered
3/4 teaspoon salt
1/4 teaspoon pepper
1 package (12 ounces) mostaccioli
2 tablespoons butter, melted
Grated Parmesan cheese

Peel eggplant and slice 1/4 inch thick. Sprinkle with salt and place in colander. Press eggplant down with a heavy plate and drain for 1 hour. Rinse and pat dry with paper towels. Dip eggplant in flour and fry a few pieces at a time in olive oil over medium-high heat. Adding oil as needed, continue frying eggplant until golden brown. Put on a plate lined with paper towels and set aside.

On medium-low heat sauté bacon, onions, and garlic in 4 tablespoons olive oil for 10 minutes. Add tomatoes, red pepper, salt, and pepper; cook for 25 minutes and set aside.

Cook mostaccioli according to package directions; drain and toss with melted butter. Grease a 3-quart baking dish. Add 1/2 of the mostaccioli, 1/2 of eggplant slices, Parmesan cheese, and 1/2 of sauce. Repeat layers and top with cheese. Cover with foil and bake at 350°F for 30 minutes. Makes 8 (1-1/4 cup) servings.

VEGETABLE VARIATIONS

LEMON BROCCOLI FETTUCCINE

This very light pasta dish is one of my most popular recipes and perfect as a first course or side dish.

1 package (10 ounces) fettuccine
5 cups broccoli flowerettes
1 cup whipping cream
4 teaspoons grated lemon peel
1/2 teaspoon salt
2 tablespoons butter, softened
2 tablespoons grated Parmesan cheese
2 tablespoons chopped parsley, preferably Italian

Cook fettuccine in 5 quarts rapidly boiling, salted water for 3 minutes. Add broccoli to fettuccine and cook another 5 minutes. Heat cream in a 10-inch frying pan over medium-high heat until bubbling. Add lemon peel and salt; boil for 30 seconds. Reduce heat to low; add drained broccoli/fettuccine, butter, Parmesan cheese, and parsley. Toss until fettuccine is evenly coated. Makes 6 (1 cup) servings.

NOODLES ASPARAGUS

Asparagus, prosciutto, and noodles are a perfect combination and a complete meal in itself.

1/3 cup butter
1-1/2 tablespoons olive oil
3/4 cup chopped onion
5 slices (2 ounces) prosciutto, chopped
3/4 cup water
2 chicken bouillon cubes
1 pound asparagus, cut into 1-inch pieces
1 package (12 ounces) tenderthin long noodles
3/4 cup half and half
1/2 cup grated Parmesan cheese
Freshly ground pepper

Heat butter and olive oil in a 2-quart saucepan over medium heat. Sauté onion until golden (do not brown). Add prosciutto and sauté briefly. Stir in water, bouillon cubes, and asparagus. Bring to a boil, reduce heat, and simmer approximately 15 minutes.

Cook tenderthin noodles according to package directions; drain. Return noodles to pot. Add asparagus mixture and half and half. Cook over medium-low heat until warmed through. Toss with 1/4 cup of Parmesan cheese. Top with remaining cheese and pepper before serving. Makes 5 (1-1/2 cup) servings.

PASTA WITH BROCCOLI

Here is an everyday dish for a meatless meal.

1 bunch broccoli
3/4 cup olive oil
1 cup chopped onions
1 package (12 ounces) tenderthin long noodles
Salt and pepper
Grated Parmesan cheese

Cook broccoli until crisp-tender, about 5 minutes. Rinse with cold water and set aside. In hot olive oil sauté onions until soft and golden. Cut broccoli into bite-size pieces and add to onions. Sauté 3 minutes and remove from heat. Cook tenderthin noodles according to package directions; drain. Toss noodles in pan with onions and broccoli. Salt and pepper to taste. Sprinkle with Parmesan cheese. Makes 6 (1-1/3 cup) servings.

VEGETABLE SPAGHETTINI

A combination of spring and winter vegetables makes a delightful pasta dish.

1/4 pound mushrooms, sliced
1 cup cauliflower, cut up
2 cups asparagus, cut up
1/2 medium onion, chopped
1 clove garlic, minced
1/4 cup butter
1 cup half and half
1 teaspoon dried sweet basil leaves
1/2 package (6 ounces) egg spaghettini
3 ounces snow peas
1/2 cup grated Parmesan cheese
Salt and pepper

Prepare vegetables. Sauté onion and garlic in butter. Add half and half and basil. Heat to boiling. Cook egg spaghettini according to package directions. During the last 6 minutes of cooking, add mushrooms, cauliflower, and asparagus. During the last 2 minutes of cooking, add snow peas; drain. Combine egg spaghettini with sauce; stir in cheese. Salt and pepper to taste. Makes 6 (1 cup) servings.

MACADAMIA MEDLEY

From the island of Hawaii, my nephew Paul and his wife, Anita, have combined macadamia nuts from their Paauhau Plantation with pasta and fresh vegetables.

> 1 medium zucchini, sliced
> 6 ounces snow peas
> 1/2 package (5 ounces) frozen petite peas, thawed
> 6 stalks asparagus, cut diagonally into 1-inch pieces or
>   1 cup broccoli flowerettes
> 12 large mushrooms, sliced
> 1 package (12 ounces) egg spaghettini
> 1 tablespoon finely minced garlic
> 2 tablespoons olive oil
> 1/2 cup butter
> 3 medium tomatoes, coarsely chopped
> 1/4 cup chopped parsley
> 1 tablespoon dried sweet basil leaves
> Salt and pepper
> 1 cup whipping cream
> 3/4 cup Parmesan cheese
> 1/3 cup chopped macadamia nuts

Prepare vegetables. Cook egg spaghettini in 5 quarts of rapidly boiling, salted water for 6 minutes. Add zucchini, snow peas, peas, asparagus, and mushrooms; cook another 6 minutes. In saucepan, over low heat, sauté garlic in 1 tablespoon oil and 3 tablespoons butter for 3 minutes. Add tomatoes, parsley, basil, and a sprinkling of salt and pepper; cook 5 to 8 minutes.

While egg spaghettini is cooking, melt remaining butter with 1 tablespoon oil and whipping cream on serving platter in 250°F oven.

Drain egg spaghettini and vegetables; toss in cream mixture, Parmesan cheese, and macadamia nuts. Top with tomato sauce. Makes 6 (2 cup) servings.

VEGETABLE VARIATIONS

VERMICELLI AL PESTO

Pesto sauce should be made with fresh sweet basil leaves, but I couldn't find them one day and used spinach and parsley leaves instead. The result was outstanding! Besides, the flavor is not as strong with spinach as it is with fresh sweet basil leaves.

1 package (16 ounces) vermicelli
1 cup packed, fresh spinach leaves
1/2 cup packed parsley leaves
2 tablespoons dried sweet basil leaves
1 cup Bertolli olive oil
1 to 2 large cloves garlic
1/2 cup pine nuts or walnuts
1 teaspoon salt
1/2 teaspoon pepper
3/4 cup grated Parmesan cheese

Cook vermicelli according to package directions; drain, reserving a small amount of pasta water. Combine remaining ingredients in food processor or blender. Blend until smooth. If pesto is too thick, stir in 1 to 4 tablespoons reserved pasta water. Toss pasta with pesto. Makes 8 (1 cup) servings.

SQUASH AND SPINACH FETTUCCINE

This pasta dish, combining spaghetti squash and green fettuccine, has an interesting and unique flavor. This recipe also offers an easy way to cook spaghetti squash.

2 tablespoons olive oil
1/2 cup chopped onion
2 cloves garlic, minced
1 can (14-1/2 ounces) peeled tomatoes
1 can (15 ounces) marinara or spaghetti sauce
1 tablespoon chopped parsley
1/2 teaspoon dried sweet basil leaves
1 spaghetti squash (2 pounds)
1 package (12 ounces) spinach fettuccine

In olive oil, sauté onion and garlic until onions are soft but not browned. Add tomatoes, marinara sauce, parsley, and basil, and cook for 25 minutes. Cut spaghetti squash in half and clean out seeds. Cook in 5 quarts boiling, salted water for 13 minutes. Add spinach fettuccine, and cook another 7 minutes. Drain fettuccine and squash. Scrape pulp from squash with fork; toss with fettuccine. Top with sauce and mix well. Makes 8 (1 cup) servings.

LINGUINE WITH FRESH TOMATO SAUCE

Prepare this linguine recipe when those beautiful, red, ripe tomatoes are in the market.

> 2 pounds large fresh tomatoes
> 1 tablespoon lemon juice
> 1/4 cup minced fresh parsley
> 1/2 teaspoon salt
> 1/8 teaspoon pepper
> 1/2 package (8 ounces) linguine
> 1/2 cup olive oil
> 2 cloves garlic, minced
> 1/2 cup sliced green onion
> 1 cup sliced fresh mushrooms
> 1/2 teaspoon Italian herbs
> Grated Parmesan cheese (optional)

Blanch tomatoes in 5 quarts boiling, salted water until skins crack; remove tomatoes with slotted spoon, reserving water. Peel and dice tomatoes; mix with lemon juice, parsley, salt, and pepper. Cook linguine according to package directions in the reserved boiling water; drain. In hot olive oil, sauté garlic, onion, mushrooms, and herbs. Add tomato mixture to oil and heat to boiling, but do not cook. Toss cooked linguine with tomato sauce. Serve with Parmesan cheese, if desired. Makes 5 (1 cup) servings.

PASTA PISELLI

Mama often made this pasta dish while I was growing up. When peas are tender, you can add 1/4 pound of diced boiled ham for variation.

1 cup coarsley chopped onion
3 tablespoons olive oil
2 cups fresh or 1 package (10 ounces) frozen
    petite peas
1/2 cup water
1 teaspoon salt
1/4 teaspoon pepper
1 package (12 ounces) salad macaroni
Grated, dry Monterey Jack or Parmesan cheese

Sauté onion in olive oil for 2 minutes. Add peas, water, salt, and pepper. Cover and cook until peas are tender, about 10 minutes. Cook salad macaroni according to package directions; drain. Toss gently with pea mixture. Sprinkle with dry Monterey Jack cheese. Makes 6 (1 cup) servings.

STIR-FRY VEGETABLES

Stir-fried vegetables are so colorful and delicious with pasta.

1/2 pound eggplant, cubed
3/4 cup olive oil
1 cup onion, thick slices, 1-1/2 inches long
2 cloves garlic, minced
1 green pepper, cubed
1 carrot, shredded
2 cups broccoli flowerettes
1/2 cup sliced green olives
1/2 teaspoon salt
1/4 teaspoon pepper
1 teaspoon oregano
1 pound ripe tomatoes, peeled and cubed
1/2 package (8 ounces) vermicelli

In a 4-quart saucepot, sauté eggplant for 5 minutes in 1/2 cup hot olive oil. Add onions and garlic; stir and cook another 3 minutes. Add 1/4 cup of olive oil to pot along with green pepper, carrot, broccoli, green olives, salt, pepper, and oregano; stir-fry for 5 minutes. Add tomatoes, stir, and cook another 2 minutes.

Cook vermicelli according to package directions; drain. Toss pasta with vegetables. Makes 4 (2 cup) servings.

LINGUINE WITH FRESH GREEN BEANS

Be sure to use fresh green beans with this good vegetarian pasta dish.

> 1 pound green beans, cut in 2-inch pieces, diagonally
> 1 package (16 ounces) linguine
> 3 tablespoons olive oil
> 1 clove garlic, minced
> 1 jar (2 ounces) sliced pimiento
> 1/4 teaspoon salt
> 1/8 teaspoon crushed red pepper
> 1 cup whipping cream
> 2 egg yolks
> 2 tablespoons butter
> 2 tablespoons Parmesan cheese
> 6 ounces fontina cheese, shredded

In 5 quarts of boiling, salted water, cook green beans for approximately 9 minutes or until tender. Remove beans from water with slotted spoon and set aside. Cook linguine according to package directions.

In hot olive oil sauté garlic, green beans, pimiento, salt, and red pepper for 5 minutes. In large bowl stir together whipping cream, egg yolks, butter, and Parmesan and fontina cheeses. Drain linguine. Toss with cream mixture and top with sautéed green beans. Makes 4 (2 cup) servings.

VERMICELLI SAUCED WITH HERBS

*This pasta recipe is an easy first course or side dish with at-home
ingredients.*

1 package (16 ounces) vermicelli
2 cloves garlic, minced
3/4 cup olive oil
1/2 teaspoon oregano
1/2 teaspoon dried sweet basil leaves
1/2 teaspoon thyme
1/4 teaspoon salt
1/8 teaspoon pepper
1/4 cup chopped parsley
1/2 cup grated Parmesan cheese
Grated Parmesan cheese

Cook vermicelli according to package directions; drain. Heat
garlic in olive oil over low heat. Stir in oregano, basil, thyme,
salt, pepper, and cooked vermicelli. Place on serving platter and
toss in parsley and Parmesan cheese. Top with additional
Parmesan cheese. Makes 5 (1-1/3 cup) servings.

RED PEPPER AND GARLIC SPAGHETTINI SAUTÉ

For the true pasta lover, here is a simple Italian dish.

1 package (12 ounces) egg spaghettini
4 large cloves garlic, minced
1/2 teaspoon crushed red pepper
1 tablespoon minced parsley
3/4 cup olive oil
Grated Romano or Parmesan cheese

Cook egg spaghettini according to package directions; drain. On low heat sauté garlic, red pepper, and parsley in olive oil. Do not brown garlic. In pan toss mixture with drained spaghettini and top with Romano cheese. Makes 5 (1 cup) servings.

BUTTERFLIES WITH EGGPLANT

Made with either butterflies or bow ties, this is a light, tasty eggplant dish.

1 eggplant (about 12 ounces) cut into 2-inch strips
1/4 pound mushrooms, sliced
1 cup sliced celery
1 teaspoon crushed, dried sweet basil leaves
2 ripe medium tomatoes, peeled and chopped
1/2 teaspoon salt
1/8 teaspoon pepper
1/2 package (5 ounces) bow ties or butterflies
6 ounces Monterey Jack cheese, cubed

In a 10-inch, nonstick frying pan, combine eggplant, mushrooms, celery, and basil; cover and steam for 10 minutes or until vegetables are limp. Add tomatoes, salt, and pepper; simmer, covered, for 15 minutes. Cook bow ties according to package directions; drain. Stir bow ties and Monterey Jack cheese in vegetable mixture. Cover and let sit 1 to 2 minutes until cheese is melted. Stir and serve. Makes 6 (1 cup) servings.

PASTA PRIMAVERA

Spring vegetables and ham make this dish sensational.

1 medium onion, chopped
1 large clove garlic, minced
1/2 cup (1 stick) unsalted butter
4 tablespoons oil
1 cup small broccoli flowerettes
1 carrot, halved lengthwise, cut diagonally into
    1/8-inch slices
1 pound thin asparagus, cut diagonally into 1/2-inch
    slices, tips left intact
1/2 pound mushrooms, thinly sliced
5 green onions, sliced in 1/4-inch slices
2 thin slices cooked ham, cut into thin strips
Salt and pepper
1 pound (16 ounces) spaghetti
3/4 cup grated Parmesan cheese

In large skillet, sauté onion and garlic in butter and oil about 2 minutes until softened, but not browned. Add broccoli, carrot, asparagus, mushrooms, and green onions and cook until crisp-tender, about 10 minutes. Add ham and salt and pepper to taste; cook 1 minute. Cook spaghetti according to package directions; drain. Add vegetables and cheese and toss until well mixed. Makes 5 (2 cup) servings.

VERMICELLI SICILIAN STYLE

When I toured Sicily with my husband, we found that eggplant was almost always on a pasta dish. What a marvelous vegetable.

1 eggplant (about 1-1/4 pounds)
Salt
1/2 cup olive oil
2 cloves garlic, minced
2 pounds ripe tomatoes, peeled and diced
1/4 teaspoon salt
1/2 teaspoon pepper
1 teaspoon dried sweet basil leaves
2 medium, red bell peppers
1/2 cup pitted ripe olives, halved
1 tablespoon pickled capers, rinsed
1/2 cup dry vermouth
1 pound (16 ounces) vermicelli
Grated Parmesan cheese (optional)

Peel eggplant and slice 1/4 inch thick. Sprinkle with salt and let drain in colander for 1 hour. Rinse and pat dry. In a large skillet, heat half of the olive oil and sauté garlic. Add tomatoes, salt, pepper, and basil. Cover and simmer for 20 minutes. Cut red peppers and eggplant into strips. In another skillet, heat remaining oil. Add peppers and sauté 5 minutes; add eggplant, olives, and capers. Sauté 5 to 8 minutes, until eggplant is tender. Combine both mixtures and add wine; cover and simmer 5 minutes.

Cook vermicelli according to package directions; drain. Toss with hot sauce. Sprinkle with Parmesan cheese, if desired. Makes 8 (1-1/2 cup) servings.

SPAGHETTI WITH TOMATOES AND BASIL

This delicious dish should be made when fresh, ripe tomatoes and fresh basil are in season.

2 pounds fresh, ripe tomatoes
1/2 cup fresh sweet basil leaves, torn
1/2 teaspoon salt
1/4 teaspoon pepper
1/3 cup pine nuts
1 tablespoon butter
1 clove garlic, minced
2 tablespoons olive oil
1 package (12 ounces) thin spaghetti
Grated Parmesan cheese

Blanch tomatoes in boiling water, peel, and cut in chunks. Add basil, salt, and pepper to tomatoes and set aside. Sauté pine nuts in butter until lightly golden, about 2 to 3 minutes. Drain butter and set aside. Sauté garlic in olive oil until soft but not brown. Add tomatoes and basil mixture and toss until well blended. Cook thin spaghetti according to package directions; drain. Toss with fresh tomato mixture and pine nuts. Sprinkle with Parmesan cheese. Makes 5 (1-1/3 cup) servings.

TWISTEES DEDOMENICO

This family recipe provides an easy, elegant first course to a meal.

1 package (12 ounces) twistee egg noodles
1/2 cup butter
2/3 cup heavy whipping cream
1 cup grated Parmesan cheese
Freshly ground black pepper

Cook twistee noodles according to package directions; drain. While twistees are cooking, melt butter with cream in 250°F oven. On platter toss twistees with butter mixture and 2/3 of Parmesan cheese until every strand is well coated. Sprinkle with remaining cheese and freshly ground pepper. Makes 6 (1 cup) servings.

FETTUCCINE ALFREDO

The dash of nutmeg makes the difference with this fettuccine recipe.

1 package (10 ounces) fettuccine
1/2 cup butter
3/4 cup half and half
1/8 teaspoon pepper
Dash nutmeg
3/4 cup grated Parmesan cheese

Cook fettuccine according to package directions; drain. Melt butter; stir in half and half, pepper, and nutmeg. On warm platter, toss cooked fettuccine, butter sauce, and Parmesan cheese. Makes 6 (1 cup) servings.

BUTTERED NOODLES WITH FRESH SAGE

Fresh sage, which is very different from dried sage, must be used in this recipe.

> **1 package (12 ounces) fine egg noodles**
> **1/2 cup butter**
> **6 fresh sage leaves**
> **Grated Parmesan cheese**

Cook noodles according to package directions; drain. Melt butter; simmer sage leaves 5 minutes. Toss with noodles. Top with Parmesan cheese. Makes 6 (1 cup) servings.

PASTA AND BEANS

My brother Vic's wife, Helen, gave me this delicious, old Italian favorite. Vic says, "It's one of my early marrige recipes that I've never tired of." This meal is great on a cold winter night and very economical.

1 cup small red beans
4 cups cold water
1 teaspoon salt
1/4 cup olive oil
1 clove garlic, minced
1/4 pound bacon, cut up
1/2 cup chopped onion
1 cup chopped celery
1-1/2 cups salad macaroni
1/2 pound fresh tomatoes, peeled and cut in chunks
1/4 teaspoon crushed red pepper (optional), or black
     pepper to taste
1/4 teaspoon oregano
1/2 cup chopped parsley
Grated Parmesan cheese

Soak beans overnight in 4 cups cold water. Drain. Cook beans in 4 cups cold water with 1 teaspoon of salt. Bring to boil and simmer 30 minutes or until tender. In hot olive oil sauté garlic, bacon, onion, and celery for 5 minutes. Add cooked beans and water and simmer another 15 minutes.

Cook salad macaroni according to package directions; drain. Add cooked salad macaroni, tomatoes, red pepper, oregano, and parsley to beans. Stir and simmer 15 minutes. Serve in soup bowls, topped with Parmesan cheese. Makes 4 (2 cup) servings.

QUICK MACARONI AND CHEESE

For a fast, easy and all time favorite, try this macaroni and cheese recipe.

1/2 package (8 ounces) elbow macaroni
3/4 pound sharp Cheddar cheese, shredded
1 can (13 ounces) evaporated milk
1/4 teaspoon Worcestershire sauce
Salt and pepper

Cook elbow macaroni according to package directions; drain. Combine cheese, milk, and Worcestershire sauce in saucepan; heat and stir until smooth. Take care not to overheat. Cheese and milk can also be heated in microwave oven at medium heat for 5 minutes. Toss sauce with elbow macaroni. Salt and pepper to taste. Makes 5 (1 cup) servings.

NOODLES WITH 4 CHEESES

My niece Claudia went to school in Florence, Italy, and speaks Italian fluently. While in Italy, she tasted many delicious pasta dishes, and this is one of her favorites.

2 ounces Gruyere
2 ounces baby Gouda
2 ounces fontina
2 ounces Gorgonzola
2 cups of milk
2 tablespoons flour mixed with 1/4 cup water
Salt and pepper
1 package (12 ounces) medium egg noodles
1/4 cup finely chopped parsley
Grated Parmesan cheese

Cut cheeses into fine pieces. Boil the milk and mix immediately with the combined flour and water. Stir cheeses in milk mixture. Salt and pepper to taste. Cook noodles according to package directions; drain. Pour sauce over noodles and mix well. Sprinkle with parsley and Parmesan cheese. Makes 7 (1 cup) servings.

FETTUCCINE GORGONZOLA

To make this dish outstanding, be sure to use the mild Gorgonzola.

5 tablespoons butter
1/2 cup pine nuts
1-1/4 cups whipping cream
4 ounces mild Gorgonzola cheese, softened
1/2 cup grated Parmesan cheese
1/3 cup chopped fresh basil leaves
1 package (10 ounces) fettuccine

Melt 1 tablespoon butter in a small saucepan, on low heat; sauté pine nuts until golden, about 2-3 minutes. Remove pine nuts. To same saucepan, add 4 tablespoons butter, whipping cream, Gorgonzola cheese, Parmesan cheese, and basil leaves. Cook over low heat, stirring and mashing with a wooden spoon to form a smooth, creamy sauce, about 5 minutes. Stir in pine nuts.

Cook fettuccine according to package directions; drain. Toss with cheese sauce. Makes 6 (1 cup) servings.

CRISPY BOW TIES

Here is a perfect chip for dipping, made with pasta. For a sweet taste, sprinkle deep-fried bow ties with sugar and cinnamon.

1 package (10 ounces) bow ties
Peanut oil

Cook bow ties according to package directions; drain and rinse in cold water and drain again. Pat dry with paper towels; let air dry for 15 minutes.

In a deep fryer or in 3 inches of hot peanut oil, drop a few bow ties at a time and cook 2 to 3 minutes, until lightly browned. Remove with slotted spoon and drain on paper towels. Let cool. Serve as a chip with a soft dip, such as herb, guacamole, or onion dip.

OLD-FASHIONED BAKED MACARONI AND CHEESE

Although an everyday dish, a pasta cookbook wouldn't be complete without it.

4 tablespoons butter
3 tablespoons flour
1/2 teaspoon salt
1/4 teaspoon white pepper
1/2 teaspoon dry mustard
3 cups milk
2 dashes cayenne pepper
2 dashes paprika
12 ounces grated, sharp Cheddar cheese
8 ounces cut macaroni

Topping
1 tablespoon melted butter
1/4 cup dry bread crumbs
1/8 teaspoon paprika

Melt butter in saucepan over low heat; blend in flour, salt, pepper, and mustard. Add milk, cayenne pepper, and paprika. Cook, stirring constantly, until sauce comes to a boil. Remove sauce from heat; stir in cheese until melted. Cook cut macaroni according to package directions; drain. Return to saucepot and combine with cheese sauce. Place in a 2-quart, greased casserole. Blend melted butter, bread crumbs, and paprika and sprinkle over macaroni. Bake in 350°F oven, 25 to 30 minutes. Makes 4 (1-1/2 cup) servings.

CREAMY GNOCCHI GORGONZOLA

Light bechamel sauce with Gorgonzola cheese is perfect for a first course dish.

3 tablespoons butter
2 tablespoons flour
2 cups hot milk
3 ounces Gorgonzola cheese, broken up
Salt and pepper
1 package (12 ounces) gnocchi
Grated Parmesan cheese
1/2 cup chopped walnuts

In saucepan, melt butter. Remove from heat and whisk in flour. Return to low heat and cook approximately 3 minutes, stirring constantly. Remove from heat and stir in hot milk. Return to medium heat, stirring constantly, until sauce thickens and boils for 1 minute. Add Gorgonzola cheese and stir until melted. Salt and pepper to taste.

Cook gnocchi according to package directions; drain. Toss with cheese sauce and top with Parmesan cheese and chopped walnuts. Makes 8 (2/3 cup) servings.

PEACHY NOODLES

You will be surprised how delicious this dessert is. Peachy noodles is one of the dishes I demonstrate to prove the versatility of pasta.

1/2 package (6 ounces) fine egg noodles
1/4 cup butter, melted
2 cans (16 ounces each) Elberta peaches, drained
2 eggs
1/2 cup sugar
1/2 cup plus 2 tablespoons sliced almonds
1 can (21 ounces) peach pie filling
1 tablespoon butter, melted
Whipped cream (optional)

Cook noodles according to package directions; drain. Toss with 1/4 cup melted butter. In food processor or blender, puree Elberta peaches, eggs, and sugar for 30 seconds. Mix cooked noodles, peach mixture, and 1/2 cup almonds. Pour into a 2-quart baking dish. Spoon pie filling over top. Toss remaining sliced almonds in butter; sprinkle over top.

Bake at 375°F, 45 to 50 minutes. Serve slightly warm. Top with whipped cream, if desired. Makes 10 (3/4 cup) servings.

RICOTTA NOODLE PUDDING

This recipe is a little more involved, but the end result is beautiful.

2 cups (3 ounces) fine egg noodles
2-1/2 cups ricotta cheese
1/3 cup almond paste
6 tablespoons butter, melted
4 eggs, separated
4 tablespoons rum
1/2 cup finely chopped, mixed glazed fruit
Grated rind of 1 lemon
1/2 cup flour
1 cup powdered sugar
1/4 teaspoon cinnamon
1/2 cup apricot jam
Candied fruit
Almond slices

Cook noodles according to package directions; drain. Mix ricotta cheese and almond paste thoroughly; add butter, egg yolks, 2 tablespoons of the rum, cooked noodles, glazed fruit, and lemon rind. Sift flour with sugar and cinnamon; stir into cheese mixture. Beat egg whites until stiff but not dry. Fold 1/4 of egg whites into cheese mixture; fold in remaining egg whites. Pour batter into a greased 6-cup fluted mold. Bake at 350°F, 45 minutes or until done. Partially cool in mold; turn onto serving plate.

Glaze with 1/2 cup apricot jam thinned with remaining 2 tablespoons heated rum. Strain glaze and brush onto pudding. Garnish with candied fruit and almond slices. Chill. Makes 8 servings.

NOODLES UPSIDE DOWN

This pasta dessert is an interesting version of the traditional upside-down cake.

1/2 package (6 ounces) fine egg noodles
2 eggs, beaten
1/2 cup sour cream
1/4 cup sugar
1/2 cup cottage cheese
1/2 teaspoon vanilla
1/4 teaspoon cinnamon
Pinch of salt
1/2 cup raisins
1/4 cup butter, melted
1 cup packed brown sugar
1 cup pecan halves
Whipped cream (optional)

Cook noodles according to package directions; drain and rinse in cold water. Combine eggs, sour cream, sugar, cottage cheese, vanilla, cinnamon, salt, and raisins. Fold into noodles. Coat bottom of an 8-inch square pan with butter. Sprinkle with brown sugar and pecans. Spread noodle mixture on top. Bake at 375°F, 45 minutes. Cool 10 minutes; invert pan onto serving dish. Serve warm. Top with whipped cream, if desired. Makes 8 servings.

SPICY APPLE NOODLE BAKE

A Florentine-style dessert, this pasta recipe, buttered and baked with apple sauce, almonds, and raisins, is delicious!

1/2 package (6 ounces) fine or medium noodles
1/4 cup butter, melted
3 cups applesauce
2 eggs
3/4 cup dark brown sugar, packed
1 teaspoon vanilla
3/4 teaspoon cinnamon
1 cup raisins
1/2 cup chopped almonds
Whipped cream

Cook noodles according to package directions; drain. Toss noodles with melted butter. Combine applesauce, eggs, brown sugar, vanilla, cinnamon, raisins, and almonds; fold into noodles. Pour into a buttered 8-inch square pan. Bake at 375°F, 45 minutes. Serve warm, topped with cream. Makes 9 servings.

NOODLE KUGEL

My sister-in-law Lois also uses this dessert recipe as a meat accompaniment by cutting the sugar in half.

1/2 package (6 ounces) medium egg noodles
1/2 cup butter, melted
1 cup sugar
1 cup (8 ounces) cottage cheese
4 eggs, beaten
1 cup (8 ounces) sour cream
1 teaspoon vanilla
2 teaspoons cinnamon
1 can (6 ounces) frozen orange juice concentrate,
  thawed
2 small, tart cooking apples, peeled and cut in
  small chunks
Whipped cream (optional)

Cook noodles according to package directions; drain. Toss with melted butter and sugar. Beat cottage cheese in blender or food processor until creamy. Add cottage cheese, eggs, sour cream, vanilla, cinnamon, orange juice, and apples to cooked noodles. Mix well; place mixture in a 2-quart, greased baking dish. Bake at 350°F for 50 minutes. Spoon into small bowls and top with whipped cream, if desired. Makes 10 (3/4 cup) servings.

Glossary

bechamel—a white sauce, sometimes enriched with cream

Bel Paese—a mild, soft, creamy cheese in a firm rind

cacciatore—an Italian dish cooked with tomatoes and herbs and sometimes wine

capellini—a very thin vermicelli, referred to as "fine hairs;" also known as angel's hair

carbonara—a pasta dish made with a white sauce that includes bits of bacon and ham

cioppino—a dish of fish and shellfish usually cooked with tomatoes, wine, spices, and herbs

egg tagliarini—a long, flat, thin noodle; the word is derived from the Italian verb, *tagliare,* "to cut"

fettuccine—a pasta in the form of narrow ribbons; a dish of which fettuccine forms the base

fontina—a cheese that is semisoft to hard in texture and mild to medium sharp in flavor

frittata—an unfolded omelet often containing chopped vegetables or meats

gnocchi—a shell-shaped macaroni made to resemble a dumpling; also known as an Italian dumpling

Gorgonzola—an Italian, pungent blue cheese

Gruyere—a firm Swiss cheese with small holes and a nutty flavor that is often used in cooking

lasagna—broad, flat noodles; a baked dish consisting of layers of boiled lasagna noodles, cheese, and a sauce of tomatoes and usually meat

linguine—a thin, flat pasta

macaroni—a pasta shaped in the form of slender tubes

manicotti—a tubular pasta shell that may be stuffed with ricotta or a meat mixture; also a pasta dish, usually with tomato sauce

marinara sauce—a sauce made with tomatoes, onions, garlic, and spices

mescolanza—a mixture or blend

minestrone—a rich, thick vegetable soup, usually consisting of dried beans and pasta, such as macaroni or vermicelli

Monterey Jack—a semisoft, whole-milk cheese with high moisture content

mortadella—a large smoked sausage made of beef, pork, and pork fat and seasoned with pepper and garlic

mostaccioli—a pasta in the shape of long tubes or ridges

mozzarella—a stringy, pully Italian cheese that is very pungent

pancetta—Italian bacon

Parmesan—a very hard, dry, sharply flavored cheese that is sold grated or in wedges

parmigiano—a dish made or covered with Parmesan cheese

pesto—a sauce consisting primarily of fresh basil, garlic, oil, pine nuts, and grated cheese

prosciutto—a dry-cured, spiced Italian ham, usually sliced thin

ravioli—a pasta in the form of little cases of dough containing a savory filling, either meat or cheese; a dish consisting of ravioli in a tomato sauce

ricotta—a white, unripened whey cheese of Italy that resembles cottage cheese; a similar cheese made in the United States from whole or skim milk

rigatoni—a macaroni made in short curved, fluted or grooved pieces

Romano— a hard, sharp Italian cheese that is often served grated

rotelle—a spiral-shaped pasta known as "small wheels"

scaloppini—thin slices of meat sauteed or coated with flour and fried

spaghetti—a pasta made in thin, solid strings

spaghettini—a pasta thinner than spaghetti but thicker than vermicelli

tetrazzini—an Italian dish prepared with pasta and a white sauce seasoned with sherry and served au gratin

verdura—Italian word for vegetables

vermicelli—a pasta made in long, solid strings, smaller in diameter than spaghetti

zitoni—a large version of ziti (tubed macaroni) with the rigati (grooved) form; also known as "husky bridegroom"

Index